EDUCATE

ENTERTAIN

EMPOWER

Jennifer
Be successful!
Nice meeting you!

HOW TO SELL

ON LINKEDIN

30 TIPS  30 DAYS

ERIK QUALMAN

BESTSELLING AUTHOR OF **SOCIALNOMICS**

HOW TO SELL ON LINKEDIN by Erik Qualman

Equalman Studios
Cambridge, MA
www.equalman.com

Cover design by Jessie Bowers and Caitlin Higgason

ISBN: 978-0-9911835-5-5 (print)
ISBN: 978-0-9911835-6-2 (ebook)

Printed in the United States of America

TABLE OF CONTENTS

# INTRODUCTION

You're busy. You have people to meet and quotas to beat. This book is here to help you sell more on LinkedIn via 30 tips in 30 days.

We are giving you tips and tools that will allow you to sell more via the art of social selling. Ironically, in order to sell more, you will need to take on the mindset of serving first. Social selling isn't about your agenda; it's about the client or customer's fears, aspirations and needs—and how you can help them succeed. If you follow the tips found in this book, you will be shocked at how effective you will be able to sell.

LinkedIn is the greatest prospecting and selling tool of our lifetime—hence why we've dedicated an entire book to it and why you are wise to read it. LinkedIn has eliminated the cold call—think about the profound sales ramifications of eliminating cold calling. For those that embrace the art and science of social selling on LinkedIn, the results are mind-blowing:

1. 45% more opportunities created

2. 80% more productive[1]

3. 80% of B2B leads come from LinkedIn[2]

4. 3x more likely to achieve sales quota

5. Directors that use LinkedIn for social selling get promoted 1.6x faster to VP[3]

6. 98% of sales reps with 5000+ LinkedIn connections achieve quota[4]

The great thing is, whether you are a LinkedIn Newbie or LinkedIn Pro, these power tips are easy and effective. Whether you are a small business, a Fortune 500 salesperson, a university trying to attract donors and students, or a non-profit organization, success is a choice in these digital times—we can only achieve success if we understand the importance of replacing the phrase *"Let's Get Ready"* with *"Let's Get Started."*

While some of the language and interfaces of LinkedIn will certainly change the moment this book is published, the social selling tips and constructs contained here are specifically designed to stand the test of time. If you don't need more sales, good for you. Feel free to use this book as a coaster—it's too small and efficient to be an effective doorstop.

For everyone else that wants to become more productive and crush their sales quotas, LET'S GET STARTED.

SECTION 1

30 POWER TIPS

1 THE 4 COMMANDMENTS OF SOCIAL SELLING

WHY

78% of social sellers outsell peers that don't use social media.[5] Whether you are a LinkedIn Newbie or Pro, you always need to start and continually revisit the basics and your baseline.

HOW

Let's start by going directly to the source—LinkedIn—to determine what they consider the four pillars of social selling:

1. **Establish Your Professional Brand:** Complete your LinkedIn profile with the customer in mind. Become a thought leader by sharing or publishing meaningful content with your connections and prospects.

2. **Find:** Research and find potential connections, prospects and customers.

3. **Engage:** Identify and share information with your connections that shows you care about and are invested in *their* success.

4. **Build Relationships:** Take the time to network before you need the network.

The 30 Power Tips in this book address these four items and beyond.

BASELINE

If you were going to start a new diet, you'd want to know your starting weight. You'd like to track how many pounds you have lost. We should do the same thing here. Also, I know some of you salespeople out there—you can't sleep at night if you don't have a goal. Let's follow the well-known mantra—if you don't set goals, you will hit them every time. Without goals, it's difficult to achieve our desired outcomes.

LinkedIn helps provide a social selling index (SSI) for free. The SSI is a score of 0-100, ranking your current social selling skill/presence. This takes 60 seconds to complete, so put this book down and do the following action item:

👍 ACTION ITEM

Take 60 seconds to pause your reading and get your SSI score here: https://www.linkedin.com/sales/ssi

Here is what it looks like:

Linked in Social Selling Index

Social Selling Dashboard   Share your SSI ☑

Erik Qualman
Motivational Speaker, CEO &
Bestselling Author

Top **1** %   Industry SSI Rank   Top **1** %   Network SSI Rank

Social Selling Index – Today
Your Social Selling Index (SSI) measures how effective you are at establishing your professional brand, finding the right people, engaging with insights, and building relationships. It is updated daily. Learn more

85
out of 100

Establish your professional brand   0 ——————— 23.15 ——— 25

Find the right people   0 —————— 17.6 —— 25

Engage with insights   0 —————— 18.98 —— 25

Build relationships   0 ————————— 25 — 25

Now that you have your score, here's a caveat: it's a good measure to look at, but it's not the only thing; it's simply one measure to help track your progress. If you have a score of 99 and haven't sold a darn thing through efforts on LinkedIn, then you aren't succeeding. Conversely, if you are crushing your quota with our LinkedIn power tips, then a low social selling index score of 19 doesn't mean so much, now does it?

Similar to the diet analogy, if you lost several pounds but it was 100% muscle weight versus fat, the scale might be telling you "hoorah!" you lost weight, but your mirror might be saying "humph" since a cubic inch of muscle weighs more than a cubic inch of fat. Ok, enough science for now—simply put, your social selling index number is just one measure of your success.

One of the world's top LinkedIn experts, Viveka von Rosen, suggests at this point making note of these numbers as well:

1. I currently have _____ connections. (https://www.linkedin.com/people/connections)

2. I currently get an average of _____ views per day/week/month. (https://www.linkedin.com/wvmx/profile)

3. I currently rank _____ in my connections. (https://www.linkedin.com/wvmx/profile/rankings)

As you implement the advice on the following pages, you will see these numbers improve.

Let's get on to more important matters. The remaining 29 tips in this book will help you use LinkedIn to sell more effectively.

2 CREATING A 100% COMPLETE & COMPELLING PROFILE

WHY

According to LinkedIn, members with completed profiles receive 40% more business opportunities. A LinkedIn profile is your resume, life story and most importantly, your personal brand. Wouldn't you want to tell your best story? Your complete story? It's amazing how many people fail to do this. Don't be one of them. Here's how to ensure your profile is as complete as it can be.

HOW

1. **Earn as many recommendations and endorsements as possible:** This social capital is invaluable. 90% of us trust what our peers say or recommend.[6] Endorsements and recommendations are the best way for others to tell your story for you.

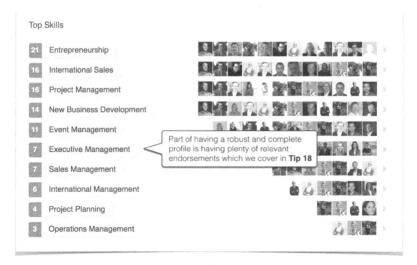

Top Skills

21	Entrepreneurship	
16	International Sales	
16	Project Management	
14	New Business Development	
11	Event Management	
7	Executive Management	
7	Sales Management	
6	International Management	
4	Project Planning	
3	Operations Management	

Part of having a robust and complete profile is having plenty of relevant endorsements which we cover in **Tip 18**

> **+👤 PRO TIP:** The easiest way to get more endorsements and recommendations is to proactively endorse and write recommendations for others.

2. **Pump up your network game:** The more connections you have, the more endorsements you will receive. According to Forbes, dig up your past, present and future.[7] Look up those old colleagues and bosses and add new acquaintances each time you make a face-to-face connection.

3. **Add a background image:** Stand out from the crowd. You wouldn't dream of having a Facebook or Twitter profile without a banner image. Don't leave your LinkedIn profile naked either. (Hat Tip: Viveka von Rosen)

4. **Don't forget the basics:** Profile picture (Tip #3), short tagline, work history and education.

5. **Brag about yourself a little:** Don't be afraid to list your awards and honors.

6. **Have a killer summary:** Combine your story into a shortened summary. This will be the first main attraction anyone will see on your page. We'll cover this in Tip #5.

7. **Post Content:** Hammer away about what you love to talk about. This gives individuals insights into your passions, personality and expertise. Clients don't buy from companies; they buy from people. Let them know who you are (more on posting content in Tip #19).

PRO TIP: According to AkkenCloud, you can make your profile even more eye-catching by creating a unique URL, constructing your headline and including your contact information.[8]

👍 **ACTION ITEM**

LinkedIn makes life easy by telling us the strength of our profile (note: this is different than our social selling index). On the right side of your profile page, you should see a "Profile Strength Ball"—the fuller the ball (with blue), the stronger your profile. Beware that LinkedIn occasionally moves the location and color of the "Profile Strength Ball." Go ahead and implement the 7 tips listed above, as well as any suggestions LinkedIn specifically recommends, to ensure your profile strength rises to the "All-Star" level.

Profile Strength

All-Star

3 PROFILE PICTURE & BANNER

WHY

You are 11 times more likely to have your profile viewed if you have a profile picture.[9] It validates who you are, because there may be others who share your same name. LinkedIn conducted an eye-tracking study and the #1 place that people look on your profile is your photo.[10]

HOW

Having an attractive social media profile picture is advantageous for both personal and professional reasons. In my interview with #1 Best Selling Author Guy Kawasaki, he calls this a "duh-ism." The duh is we all know we need an attractive profile picture. Yet, many fail to have one!

> **❝** Nothing you wear is more important than your smile. **❞**
> — Connie Stevens

Kawasaki indicates an attractive profile picture supports the narrative that you are likeable, competent and trustworthy. But how do we produce a photo that attracts people, job recruiters and new business?

According to Kawasaki, the science to producing your best headshot or profile picture is based on four key factors:

1. **Focus on your face:** There's no room for your family, dogs or company logo.

2. **Go asymmetrical:** Symmetry makes a photo less interesting. Don't put your face in the middle. Use vertical lines to divide your photo into thirds and place your eyes on one of the dividing lines (see Kawasaki's profile picture below).

3. **Face the light:** The source of light should come from in front of you.

4. **Think big:** Upload a photo that is at least 600 pixels wide. People will most often scan your posts and will see the postage size image. However, when they click on your posts or double-click on your image itself, they will see a crisp, clear and large photo of you.

Achieve an asymmetrical picture by dividing the picture into equal thirds and have one eye align with one of the dividing lines

Guy Kawasaki

BANNER IMAGES

Top selling author and LinkedIn Expert Viveka von Rosen recommends uploading a header or background image on your personal profile (current LinkedIn size is 1400 x 425). This is one of the easiest ways to distinguish your profile on LinkedIn. For example, if you work for a company or represent a product, incorporate (with permission) the branding including colors, fonts, logos, workplace photos, etc. into your header image. We also recommend adding your contact information within the graphic.

4 BOSS BUTTON

WHY

LinkedIn's default settings will automatically share your activity updates with your connections. Activity updates include listing a new job, new skill or a change in your location, etc. While sharing on LinkedIn is generally a good thing, sometimes you don't want to share certain activity updates with your connections, clients or boss.

This is where "The Boss Button" comes into play. It lets you be in control of turning these notifications on or off, making you "the boss" of your own account. If you don't want certain updates published to your network, you can adjust the settings. This allows you to update your LinkedIn profile often to help drive leads and sales without the fear of your boss thinking you are job searching...even if you are.

> Victoria, you're the boss of your account.

HOW

There are a couple of ways to be the boss of your LinkedIn updates.[11]

1. Go to your profile, then to the right sidebar. Here, LinkedIn gives you the option to notify your network by simply sliding yes or no.

Notify your network?	Notify your network?
No, do not publish an update to my network about my profile changes. `No`	**Yes**, publish an update to my network about my profile changes. `Yes`

2. Go to Settings ⇨ Privacy ⇨ Sharing Profile Edits ⇨ Toggle On or Off.

Profile privacy

Edit your public profile Change
Choose how your profile appears in search engines

Who can see your connections Change
Choose who can see your list of connections Connections

How You Rank Change
Choose whether or not to be included in this feature Yes

Viewers of this profile also viewed Change
Choose whether or not this feature appears when people view your profile Yes

Sharing profile edits Change
Choose whether your network is notified about profile changes No

Profile viewing options Change
Choose whether you're visible or viewing in private mode Private mode

Notifying connections when you're in the news Change
Choose whether we notify people in your network that you've been Yes
mentioned in an article or blog post

Sharing profile edits Close
Choose whether your network is notified about profile changes No

Should we let people know when you change your profile, make
recommendations, or follow companies?

No

+👤 PRO TIP: Know the pros and cons of sharing your profile edits to make sure you are being the boss of your LinkedIn account. The best question to ask is, "Will this update be of value to my network, prospects and clients?" Use the three-second rule. If you have to think more than three seconds about its value or appropriateness, then it's best not to share it with the world. Otherwise, share away.

5 CONSTRUCTING A KILLER SUMMARY

WHY

Your summary is one of the first things people see and read about you on LinkedIn. It's part of your first (online) impression and it's a big deal. When it comes to business, there are no longer any "blind dates."

> " Your smile is your logo, your personality is your business card, how you leave others feeling after an experience with you becomes your trademark. "
> —Jay Danzie

From a sales perspective, ensure your summary addresses the following questions:

1. How and why you are going be a helpful and valuable partner?

2. Are you likeable?

3. Are you trustworthy?

4. What makes you unique and why is that so great?

HOW

Be as likeable as possible. An easy way to be likeable is writing in a similar manner as you would speak in a face-to-face introduction.

FOR EXAMPLE

JOHN: What do you do for a living?

TYLER: I help build bridges.

Notice here that Tyler doesn't reply: *"I'm a passionately dynamic and disruptive force within building and construction. My unique skillset of time management and quality production is an innovative approach and my thought leadership is unparalleled in the field."*

Yet, so many of us write like this on LinkedIn for our summaries. Try to write as you would speak.

Continuing with our offline conversation example...

JOHN: Wow—that sounds difficult, but very cool. How did you get into that line of work?

TYLER: Funny enough it was a Lego beginner builder set I received as a gift on my 8th birthday. I've been fascinated with building ever since, especially building bridges.

JOHN: Have you contributed to any of the bridges in the city that I might know?

TYLER: I was fortunate to be a part of the teams on both the Zakim and Mackinac Bridge projects.

JOHN: Very cool.

**EXAMPLE LINKEDIN SUMMARY
WRITTEN FROM THE CONVERSATION:**

We all remember our favorite childhood birthday gift. Mine was a Lego construction builder set I received on my 8th birthday. Every day since then, I've been fascinated by the art and science of building—specifically building bridges. Starting my own bridge firm by the age of 25, we've been fortunate to collaborate with great clients and partners over the past 15 years, including the award-winning Zakim and Mackinac Bridge projects. I'm most proud of our projects being on time and under budget for our clients. My dad often likes to joke that I was "built" for this.

1. **DO NOT:** Use generic adjectives such as: responsible, unique, organized, efficient and a team player. You are not generic so do not make your summary generic.

   Instead: Use scenarios. What specific skills or experience do you have that are beneficial for partners, clients and customers?

OTHER WORDS THAT LINKEDIN INFLUENCER JEFF HADEN SUGGESTS TO AVOID:

"World-class." Usain Bolt is a world-class sprinter and has Olympic medals to prove it. Lionel Messi is a world-class soccer player and has four Ballon d'Or trophies to his name. These two are world-class, while most others are not.

"Authority." Like Margaret Thatcher said, "Power is like being a lady…if you have to tell people you are, you aren't." Show your expertise instead.

> Instead of saying the word "authority," use examples like "Presented at TEDxEast" or "Predicted 50 out of 50 states in the 2016 election"—these examples prove a level of authority without actually having to use the word.[12]

2. **DO NOT:** List controversial hobbies or interests like "I have 47 venom spitting and blinding cobras that I breed in my free time".

   Instead: List your superpowers. What separates you from the rest? From the example above, it could be specific experience/clients (*Zakim & Mackinac Bridge Projects*) or deliverables (*on-time and under-budget*).

3. **DO:** Tell a story. How did you start in your career, what was your breakthrough moment and how do your customers/clients benefit?

   Example: Kay Allison, CEO and Founder at the Energy Infuser, Inc.

BACKGROUND

 SUMMARY

"Harriet the Spy" was my Bible when I was a little girl. I copied her by spying on my neighbors and writing down what I observed in a little notebook, as well as noting questions that their behaviors triggered. I even spent a summer eating nothing but tomato sandwiches.

Today, I still "spy" on people, although these days, respondents give me their permission me to ask them nosy questions and pry into their homes.

My passion is inventing new, more powerful and profitable ways to listen creatively to consumers... and then turning the insights that emerge into business ideas that generate $50MM in annual revenue and above.

Our Passion Point Framework shows brands how to align with consumers' passions. These clients no longer have to settle for incremental growth, they enjoy exponential growth.

4. **DO:** Create your summary in a Word document to ensure you have no spelling or grammatical errors. You can add bullets and special characters to your Word document that will copy and paste into LinkedIn (Hat Tip: Viveka von Rosen).

5. **DO NOT**: Use bullets and special characters excessively.

Use your own voice and personality to construct a brand that resonates with who you are, is consistent with your company and how you would like to come across to others. Continue to revise, improve, revise, improve.

6 DEVELOPING YOUR VOICE

WHY

Determine what voice you are going to use for your profile information (e.g., summary, awards): first person, third person or a combination/neutral position.

If you are a well-known individual with many accolades, it often makes sense to write in the third person. This is similar to an author's bio at the end of their book—as you will see about this awesome author at the end of this amazing book ☺. Even though the author penned the book— the bio is usually written in third person. The downside to writing in third person is that it isn't as personal.

First person is how most of us should write on LinkedIn. Keep it short, personal and tell a story. The story should center on what is most beneficial and interesting to the reader—not what is most interesting to you.

Whatever voice you decide, the key is to keep your viewers engaged and avoid putting people to sleep with the first few sentences. Just like a good journalist, lead with the headline.

If you don't feel you have much to say—keep it short! There is beauty in brevity.

Use the 1-2-3 template below to help make your summary relevant and interesting:

1. Include an interesting fact about you—the more personal, the better. For example: Scaled Mt. Everest, performed at Carnegie Hall, won a childhood spelling bee, appeared on a game show, etc.

2. How does the above interesting fact relate to what you do today or what did you learn from this experience that will help your clients today?

3. Do you have a roster of clients, credential or a fact you can point to as proof of your skills?

EXAMPLE

When I was 25, I trekked to the North Pole—home of the Clauses. While making the voyage I thought about quitting at least 1,000 times. Honestly, it was probably closer to 5,000 times. You see, I actually don't like the cold!

This perseverance and experience helps me today—as my team and I bring the same pioneering spirit to the field of elementary education. Specifically, our award winning mobile educational learning games are dramatically increasing the development of kids' STEM skills.

Over 70% of the top-rated elementary schools in the U.S. are already using our program and we believe your students/ children would benefit from joining the community as well.

Pause now and try the 1-2-3 method yourself, or you can read a few more real-world examples we've provided before you write your own.

Shaquille O'Neal's (yes the 7'1" hall of fame basketballer) summary, although a bit long, is a good example of a showcasing a personable approach.

HOW

Shaquille O'Neal—First Person Example

 Summary

During 19 seasons in the National Basketball League, I drove success on and off the court. I developed partnerships with global brands, pursued my academic interests in business and leadership and became the only current or former NBA player to hold three degrees: a bachelor's, a master's and a doctorate.

Basketball remains a big part of my life, whether it is providing NBA analysis on TV, serving as part-owner of the Sacramento Kings or appearing as a featured character in the latest video games. Since 1985, every NBA championship team has included a current or former teammate. I guess that makes me the Kevin Bacon of basketball.

Since retiring from the basketball court, I've expanded my brand relationships into one of the most diverse portfolios in the business world. As an early adopter of technology, I've identified innovative organizations as a serial tech investor. I work with brands that are household names such as Turner Networks, Reebok, IcyHot, AT&T and many other great companies. I also bring my business acumen to like-minded companies as a featured speaker at conferences and events nationwide.

Though I'm best known for basketball and business, my interests have always varied. I've released four studio albums and served as a sworn reserve officer in several law enforcement agencies across the country. I've collaborated on everything from fashion lines and jewelry to best-selling beverages and foods; from the latest technology products and games to children's books.

Jeff Weiner, LinkedIn's CEO, takes a third person approach with information about past and current experience:

Background

 Summary

Internet executive with over 20 years of experience, including general management of mid to large size organizations, corporate development, product development, business operations, and strategy.

Currently CEO at LinkedIn, the web's largest and most powerful network of professionals.

Prior to LinkedIn, was an Executive in Residence at Accel Partners and Greylock Partners. Primarily focused on advising the leadership teams of the firm's existing consumer technology portfolio companies while also working closely with the firm's partners to evaluate new investment opportunities.

Previously served in key leadership roles at Yahoo! for over seven years, most recently as the Executive Vice President of Yahoo!'s Network Division managing Yahoo's consumer web product portfolio, including Yahoo's Front Page, Mail, Search, and Media products.

Specialties: general management, corporate development, product development, business operations, strategy, product marketing, non-profit governance

7 FINDING PROSPECTS

WHY

LinkedIn is an essential tool to deepen relationships with current clients and customers. It is also the world's largest tool to fill your sales pipeline with new prospects. It's key to note that LinkedIn connections are very valuable since they are often the gateways to prospects. As previously mentioned, 98% of sales reps with more than 5000 LinkedIn connections meet or surpass quota.[13]

One of the main reasons for social selling is because there is no longer just one buyer at a company. There are many influencers; sourcing them via LinkedIn to understand their connections and roles is critical. As LinkedIn's Mike Derezin, vice president of LinkedIn Sales Solutions, notes, "Today there are, on average, 5.4 buyers in the B2B sales process. And when you include the key influencers, there are probably closer to 10 people influencing the buying decision."[14]

HOW

Search: To find new prospects, use the *LinkedIn Advanced Search* feature to look for people that match your customer profile. You can search by title, company, industry, location, university, etc. I find it effective to search by title and then reduce this list by focusing on the universities I attended or by the city I'm living in. This gives me the best chance to have an immediate personal connection with the prospect. An added benefit of being in the same city allows me to have a face-to-face conversation sooner rather than later.

The main search bar is at the top of your profile page. To expand the search bar into an advanced search query, just simply click on the word "Advanced" next to the search box. There is also the ability to save searches. The huge benefit here is when a new prospect matches your saved search query, LinkedIn will email you. LinkedIn will actually be sending you prospects via email! Yep, it's that easy.

LinkedIn Pulse: Reading industry-related content via LinkedIn Pulse is crucial to staying on top of the competition and current trends. It can also be ideal for finding customers. Next time you read a post on LinkedIn, click the expand button to see who has either liked or commented on the post. This window makes it easy for you to discover like-minded people and prospects. Most importantly, it gives you a natural opening to begin an online conversation.[15]

> ### EXAMPLE
>
> *Hi Dave, I saw you liked the article "Funding Tips for Small Business Owners." I wanted to reach out and ask what you found most useful from the article?*
>
> *I work in finance helping early stage entrepreneurs fund their ideas and Tip #5 was my personal favorite—I've actually seen this work first hand. If you ever have any questions about finding the right kind of funding, I can help or maybe we'll bump into each other at a Crimson Tide Tailgate—Roll Tide!*
>
> A quick reminder that connecting authentically is key and will positively help your prospecting.

Find the Influencers: Identify who the influencers are within your industry, learn who is engaging with them and why. Peter Thiel, author of *Zero to One*, discusses the advantages of using a very focused or niche strategy to stay ahead of the curve in business. Below is a guide on how to use the same strategy for social selling.

1. Focus on active profiles and thought leaders in your industry and determine what they have in common: any interests, groups, skills, posts or mission statements. This will help adjust what your online profile and contributions look like. You can see what is working for most of these thought leaders and borrow items that make sense for you.

2. Look at the profiles of the people engaging with these thought leaders. Patterns and characteristics will begin to emerge and you'll soon have a new digital customer profile. Many will even ask for help from these thought leaders. Those asking questions have just self-identified a need for your product—they are literally raising their hand and saying, please sell me a solution that will help me!

3. It's not always this simple. Many in need of help will not openly ask for it. However, if you see people actively engaged around a certain challenge, it's a good bet that's the challenge they are also wrestling with.

Do More Research: Successful prospecting is driven by "the strength of your list and the precision of your targeting."[16] Spend time understanding where your current customers came from and why they're working with you. Great questions to ask your best customers over lunch are "how did you find us and why do you work with us?"

Compare your network with your competitor's network. How are they different and how do your customer bases vary? Remember that it's key to identify and understand the viewpoint of your customers. Find the most valuable item for them as a result of doing business with you and accentuate this in your social selling approach.

People Also Viewed: The "People Similar to" and "People Also Viewed" sidebars should be your best friends. These sidebars show profiles similar to those you are viewing. In essence, LinkedIn has pre-identified potential profiles that could be of interest to you. This is similar to Amazon's or Netflix's recommendation engine but for individuals on LinkedIn.

Keep an eye out for when prospects switch jobs. This is an ideal time to send a congratulatory note and follow-up. They are most likely going to try and make an immediate impact at their new job and you can be their trusted advisor to make it happen.

> ❝ People will try to tell you that all the great opportunities have been snapped up. In reality, the world changes every second, blowing new opportunities in all directions, including yours. ❞
> —Ken Hakuta

Invest in Premium Features: LinkedIn offers premium features, which can increase your odds of finding potential prospects. They come at varying cost levels, but these premium features allow you to search prospects by company size and seniority.[17] InMail allows you to send your message to any person on LinkedIn without being connected.

If needed, you can purchase an extra 10 InMails a month. Use tools like Attach.io to track engagement with your sent messages. Attach.io will tell you if a prospect opened your message, if they've forwarded your message and more.[18] The most robust tool that LinkedIn offers is Sales Navigator, which will be discussed later in the book. If you don't have the budget for the premium tools, don't fret, almost every tactic and item we recommend can be done with the free version.

> **+👤 PRO TIP:** Some salespeople I've spoken with have found that the LinkedIn Recruiter tool works best for them. That's right, the tool that is designed for job recruiting on LinkedIn is great for sales. It allows users to reach deeper into the organization and to better see the organizational structure. It is also less expensive than some of the other LinkedIn sales tools like Sales Navigator.

8 RE-ENGINEERING THE COLD CALL

WHY

90% of decision makers say they don't respond to cold outreach,[19] while conversely 80% of introductions generate a sale.[20]

HOW

Leverage your network on LinkedIn by identifying the best path for a referral or introduction into a hot prospect. Find the warmest entry path and write introductory messages that can't be ignored.

For example, say I want to connect with the CMO of Old Navy:

1. Find the Connection:

I go to the LinkedIn search bar and type "Old Navy CMO."

The profile for the CMO of Old Navy appears and, lucky for me, I'm a 2nd connection with him—meaning that I have a direct connection with Jamie Tuner and Jamie Turner has a direct connection with the CMO—YES!

> **+👤 PRO TIP:** Google search is often better than LinkedIn's search. Go to Google, type in "Old Navy CMO LinkedIn"—it will usually be the first result.

2. Get Introduced:

Get introduced by using either the 1) LinkedIn introduction link 2) LinkedIn email 3) InMail (paid) or 4) regular email (e.g., Gmail)—for more on finding emails, refer to the *Bonus Tips & Tricks* section late in this book.

Hi Jamie—

How about our Red Sox!

Loved seeing your latest promotion at Intel. I noticed you are connected with Ivan Wicksteed at Old Navy. A warm intro-duction from you would go a long way. I believe their mar-keting team would benefit from my book What Happens on Vegas Stays on YouTube. If this is a big ask and you are more comfortable giving me insights, I completely understand.

Beers soon.

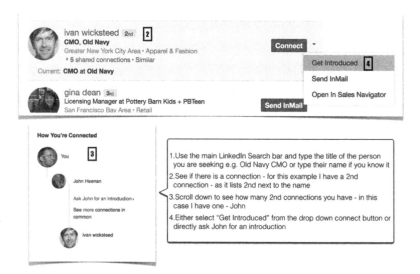

+👤 PRO TIP: Instead of simply stating "Beers soon" grab a nice image of cold beers (see below) or animated gif (short video) and insert it into the message.

Seem too aggressive? What if the person doesn't drink? Do your research to craft the best personalized message possible—for example, you may find a picture online (e.g., Facebook, Google Images, Flickr, etc.) of John drinking a beer at a Red Sox game that can give insight beyond what is listed on LinkedIn. The key to good communication lies in prior preparation and research. Still unsure? Play it safe: say *coffee soon* and display images of coffee.

+👤 PRO TIP: Generally, I prefer to use traditional email (assuming I have the email address of the person I'm asking for the introduction). Mainly because a) it is more personal, b) it usually gets a quicker response and c) many people don't know how to use LinkedIn or check it as often as they check their email.

This type of warm approach works best. Don't believe me? Let's go straight to the source itself—LinkedIn's own sales team. That's right, they need to sip their own champagne when they are selling their premium services—the LinkedIn management team demands it of the LinkedIn sales team.

Yes, the LinkedIn sales team uses the premium services they sell. What is their #1 source of revenue? <u>Warm introductions</u>. Per the chart below, 32% of LinkedIn revenue comes from warm leads. Moreover, warm leads have a 23% higher average deal size and are 37% more likely to close than other lead sources.

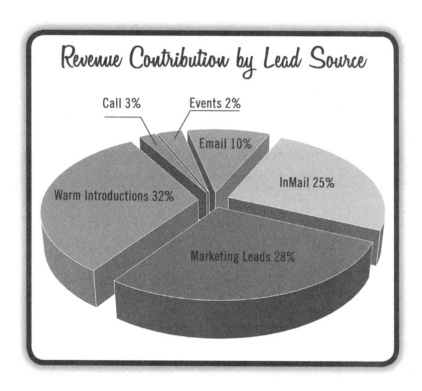

9 LISTEN FIRST, SELL LAST

I thought for this tip, it would be nice to add another voice to the mix. Writer and marketing professional Tara DeMarco pieced together this outstanding summary of a social selling webinar I did as an advisory board member for Bazaarvoice (NASDAQ: BV). Here is a transcript of her summary with a few items adjusted and infused for clarity and brevity:

Our advisor Erik Qualman, author of *Socialnomics*, compares social media to a party. If you go to a party and see a group of people talking, he explains, you wouldn't walk up and say, "Excuse me, you look like you're having a pleasant conversation. Can we talk about why I'm great for the next five minutes?"

For some reason, however, we often forget these basic social skills in the digital world.

Too many businesses and salespeople jump into LinkedIn and immediately begin selling—pushing messages about their products and brand into an already ongoing conversation. Through what he calls the "social selling circle," Erik explains the steps to effectively sell on LinkedIn or any digital gathering place.

1. **Listen.** Engage in active listening as opposed to simply waiting your turn to speak. What's being said about your brand, your products and your industry? See what people are saying before jumping in. Look at what your prospects are posting to see what is top of mind, personally and professionally. Some

post more than others but you can usually get a good feel for a person before even reaching out.

See a more detailed version of this chart in Section 2

2. **Interact.** Join the conversation in a way that adds value. You can't just talk about how wonderful you or your company are and expect people to **engage**—you have to contribute in a flow that makes sense and isn't awkward. Think of the offline world where you are having lunch and two potential prospects are enthralled about the controversial NFL game over the weekend—would you say *"Excuse me, I didn't see the game, but did you hear about the sushi chef that has been stealing money from the proprietor—we have an enterprise grade software solution that would have caught this."* Of course you wouldn't. That would be awkward—yet many of us do similar things like this when selling online.

3. **React.** Respond to what is being said about you, your brand or your company, ensuring your reply is succinct and timely. Once you have established interest, refrain from replying with the "kitchen sink" of everything you can do. Sending too much information is detrimental and will:

    a. Delay your response time, since you will be spending valuable time trying to craft an all-encompassing message.

    b. Overwhelm your prospect who will put off reading your reply until they have "enough" time to read the lengthy content.

    c. Diminish your opportunity to sprinkle new ideas and materials over the coming days because you have already sent everything. Specifically, if you have three points the prospect might be interested in, it's better to save two of them for later messages. Hence if she/he responds, you can send them additional nuggets of interest or if they don't respond, you have another excuse or reason to send them a note.

Nobody likes to receive email. The one universal question that elicits the same response across the 45 countries where I have spoken is—"Who wants to receive more email?" No one has *ever* raised his or her hand. If you despise receiving long emails, why would you expect your prospect or client to welcome a long response?!

It's also important to understand the responsibility associated with the "*React*" step. Beyond the sales team, this is where many brands and companies "drop the ball" when it comes to social selling. If 70% of people are saying they like something about your product, how quickly are you changing your product to deliver more of what they like? Insights without action are worthless.

The same holds true for negative feedback. If people are talking about what they dislike about your products or brand, how quickly are you working to fix it? For all the companies jumping into social media, most don't have a plan for acting on what they learn—their social efforts are placed into silos for a specific department. "Social" isn't a department—your entire company must be listening and reacting to online conversations to drive any real value and to increase sales.

4. **Sell.** If you're reacting to customer and prospect feedback to add value and solutions, it will feel more like collaboration and less like selling. While LinkedIn is the world's most powerful sales tool, at this point in the conversation, for many of you, this "sell" part is where you should try and setup an offline meeting. You still can't replace face-to-face interaction and attention. LinkedIn is a tool to help augment offline interactions when time and distance are an issue. When you can get an in-person meeting, you need to make it happen. LinkedIn is just a way to communicate before and between these real world meetings.

Following are two great questions that can be asked early on in the sales process. These starting questions are good for LinkedIn messaging, as well as helpful for interacting and reacting. They are also short to type!

1. *What are you most excited about in the next 12 months?*

2. *What are the challenges that might prevent you from achieving the above?*

When they respond to question #1 and #2, here are two items that correlate:

When you receive a response to question #1, ask if they have quantified dollar value or monetary opportunity related to what they are most excited about. Ex: *I too would be excited about launching vegetable-based gummy bears for kids in the top U.S. markets. Have you identified what type of revenue opportunity is associated with this?*

When they respond to the estimated dollar value—the vegetable-based gummy bear market is $250 million—ask what type of investment they would be willing to put toward it, ensuring they remove challenges to capitalize on this opportunity. Give them bands:

    a. $10,000 - $20,000

    b. $20,001 - $40,000

    c. $40,001 - $60,000

    d. $60,001 - $80,000

When receiving a response to question #2, provide a short answer on how you might be able to resolve the challenges and ask to setup an offline meeting to discuss—list three specific dates and time windows to help simplify the scheduling process. Always give the time in their time zone, not your time zone.

> **＋👤 PRO TIP:** When proposing dates and times, suggest one within the next week, one within two weeks and one in three weeks. Make sure to vary the times (morning, early afternoon and later in the day) to ensure you are taking different time zones into consideration. Don't give open-ended statements like "what day or time works for you?" This slows the process.

By asking the two questions above, you have already provided value since most people don't give these questions enough thought. Most prospects are mired in the day-to-day fire drills to truly reflect on what has them most excited. You have positioned yourself as a strategic ally with short and pointed questions rather than paragraphs of text.

> **＋👤 PRO TIP:** If your prospect is not aware of how much money they are willing to apply to their top challenge/opportunity or if they can't quantify the opportunity, it may be a signal that you are not dealing with the decision maker.

As you sell, your customers will follow this same model—hence why it's a Social Selling *CIRCLE*:

1. **Listen.** Customers/clients hear what your product or service has to offer, both by listening to what you're selling and by listening to each other on social media and in conversations offline.

2. **Interact.** They'll interact with your product or service by using them.

3. **React.** They'll react to your product, developing their own opinion of what's working and what isn't, what they like and what they dislike.

4. **Sell.** Based on their reaction, they'll sell for or against you via word of mouth. If you've done your job right by listening, interacting and reacting to feedback in order to consistently deliver better experiences and solutions—customers and clients will do the selling for you, by sharing their love of your products or service with their networks, both online and off. At this point, the Social Selling Circle continues in a positive reinforcing circle and the sales will continue to increase without additional effort on the sales side.

 **ADDING CONNECTIONS**

WHY

It's not *what* you know, it's *who* you know. The same philosophy applies online. The more quality connections you have on LinkedIn, the more likely these connections can help you achieve your goals.

> **‟** My greatest regrets are the things I did not do,
> the opportunities missed and the things unsaid. **”**
> —Jim Keller

HOW

Start by making a list of the top 20 people you would like to connect with.

1. Go to the profile page of the person you want to connect with and click the "Connect" button. Select from the dropdown list with the options of how you might know this person.

   WARNING: Do not connect from the "People you may know" section of LinkedIn. It doesn't allow you to write a custom invitation. Instead, a generic "I'd like to connect with you" note gets sent and prevents you from adding context and a personal touch to the invitation.

   According to Experian, generic messages get lower acceptance rates than messages with a personal touch[21].

NOTE: The generic message is shown in this image.

2. Above is a screen shot for the message box that will display when you go to connect with someone. LinkedIn's message box for an invite will default to a generic message and it says Include a personal note (optional)." This is not optional for top social sellers like you—take the time to complete this box. Why? It will make you stand out from the crowd. Most sales-people will not take the extra effort to personalize this message and it will cost them. That is not you—you are better than that. Take the time to write a personal message and include:

   a. The person's name

   b. A reminder about how you know them

   c. A compliment about their work, persona, company, etc.

   d. A brief explanation about the benefit they will receive from connecting with you

   e. An insight on something you have in common

3. If you have a Twitter handle, include it at the end of your message. I usually put it below my name. LinkedIn doesn't allow you to include your email, web address or phone number prior

to being connected with someone. However, they don't currently block Twitter handles. Another workaround, especially if you don't use Twitter, is to write your email like this equalman [at] gmail [dot] com

4. Remember to write in short sentences—you only have 300 words, use them wisely.

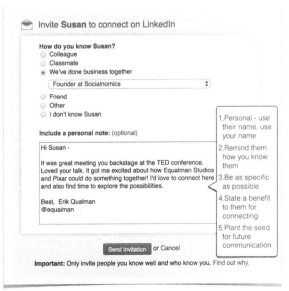

CASE STUDY: FIRST BUSINESS

● ●

CHALLENGE: First Business, a company specializing in financial advising, desired new lead sources and to shorten their sales cycle.

ACTION: First Business used some of the steps outlined in this book to locate new leads.

RESULT: As a result, the sales team's ability to go from connections to setting up meetings increased 80%. LinkedIn acted as the conduit for introductions with potential clients and increased the sales team's likelihood of getting a foot in the door. [22]

11 POSTING-IT-FORWARD

WHY
Posting-It-Forward will make you and others feel better. People will want to help you.

HOW
You have heard the expression pay it forward: performing good deeds without expecting something in return. LinkedIn makes it easy to praise someone digitally.

Make a daily habit of spending a minimum of three minutes to do any of the following:

1. Endorse someone on LinkedIn for a skill they have.

2. Send a private message with a link to an interesting article and a personal note along the lines of *"Hello Sophia. I thought of you when reading this article..."*

3. In your status updates, shine a light on others. A good guideline to start with is 9 out of 10 of your status updates should not be about you, but about others. Heap praise on others.

4. Remember the old adage from networking sage Dale Carnegie—when it comes to networking, it's more important to be interested (in other people) than to spend all your time trying to get people interested in you.

51

5. If a potential connection or prospect posts an article on LinkedIn, take the time to select the "Like" button for the article and
post a positive comment—the more specific the comment, the
better. If you have time to post a question about the article, this
will elicit a response.

> **❝** If your actions inspire others to dream more, learn more, do
> more and become more, you are a leader. **❞**
> —John Quincy Adams

Research shows that posting positive items about others increases not
only their happiness but your own happiness as well.[23] Post-It-Forward. According to *Psychology Today*, there are numerous benefits to
paying random acts of kindness forward and helping someone else in
need.[24] Specifically:

- Improves your immune system.

- By contributing towards the greater good, a person's self-worth
  and self-esteem improves.

- Encourages one to meet new people, avoid isolation and do
  new things—even if they are outside one's comfort zone.

- Positive energy flows helping to squash chronic negativity in
  the mind.

- Kindness helps relieve stress in the workplace.

> **"** Helping contributes to the maintenance of good health, and it can diminish the effect of diseases and disorders both serious and minor, psychological and physical. **"**
> —Allan Luks, after surveying 3,296 volunteers

Source: http://www.psychologytoday.com/articles/200607/pay-it-forward
http://payitforwardday.com/about/why-pay-it-forward/

 ACTION ITEM

Look for reasons to praise three people each day, expecting nothing in return. You will be amazed at the positive responses you receive.

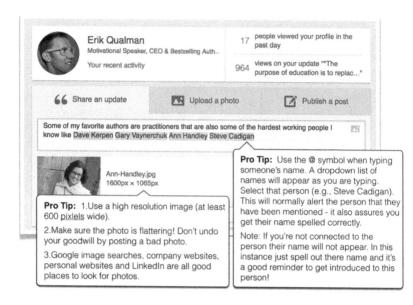

Erik Qualman
Motivational Speaker, CEO & Bestselling Auth..

Your recent activity

17 people viewed your profile in the past day

964 views on your update ""The purpose of education is to replac..."

❝❝ Share an update   📷 Upload a photo   ✏️ Publish a post

Some of my favorite authors are practitioners that are also some of the hardest working people I know like Dave Kerpen Gary Vaynerchuk Ann Handley Steve Cadigan

Ann-Handley.jpg
1600px × 1065px

Pro Tip: 1.Use a high resolution image (at least 600 pixlels wide).

2.Make sure the photo is flattering! Don't undo your goodwill by posting a bad photo.

3.Google image searches, company websites, personal websites and LinkedIn are all good places to look for photos.

Pro Tip: Use the @ symbol when typing someone's name. A dropdown list of names will appear as you are typing. Select that person (e.g., Steve Cadigan). This will normally alert the person that they have been mentioned - it also assures you get their name spelled correctly.

Note: If you're not connected to the person their name will not appear. In this instance just spell out there name and it's a good reminder to get introduced to this person!

LEARNING MOMENT

• •

I loved a particular song by Christopher Tin and wanted to use it for a YouTube video I was creating. Tin embraced the idea that I was creating awareness of his music with my loyal followers. We exchanged signed copies of books for signed copies of music and posted positive comments about one another digitally. Tin's incredible talents eventually enabled him to win two Grammy's. While we expected nothing in return by "posting it forward," each of us experienced long-term benefits.

12 INTRODUCING PEOPLE

WHY

Introducing the right people builds trust and positions you as a leader.

HOW

Here's the easiest way to introduce your LinkedIn contacts:

1. Click your "Inbox" icon (looks like a cartoon message bubble) on the top right of any LinkedIn page.

2. Click "Compose a new message" (blue circle with a pencil tab).

3. In the "To:" field, type in the names of those you'd like to introduce (note: you must be connected already and the limit is 50 people—I recommend introducing only 2 people at a time).

4. Write a personal message on why you are providing a connection and include insight on the benefit you see from the relationship.

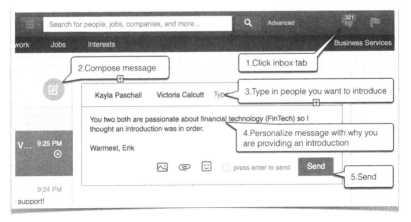

Another way to introduce people is to go to one of your contact's profiles and select "Share Profile" from the "Send a message" dropdown menu. The main benefit of this versus the introduction method noted above is that it'll send a LinkedIn connection invite with your message, allowing the users to more easily connect.

SHARING A LINKEDIN CONTACT'S PROFILE:

1. In the search bar on your LinkedIn home page, type in a contact's name and locate their profile.

2. Click their name in the results.

3. Find the blue "Send a message" button just to the right of their photo, expand the dropdown menu and select "Share Profile"

4. In the "To:" field, place the contacts you want to send this to (limit 50).

5. Don't use the generic message! Personalize why your contacts should connect.

6. Click "Send Message."

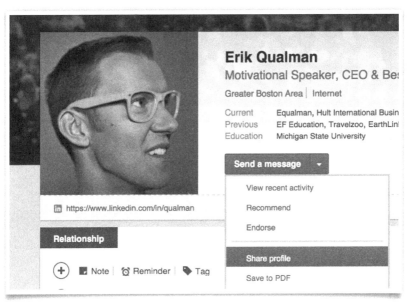

13 | ENDORSING PEOPLE

WHY

It's a way of posting-it-forward. It keeps you top of mind with important connections in a positive way. Oh, and the science shows it makes you and the recipient happier.[25]

HOW

1. Go to the profile of the person you wish to endorse.

2. Underneath their photo, you will see suggested endorsements.

3. Select the endorsement you feel is most relevant.

4. The endorsement must be genuine—only endorse people for skills you know they have. Endorsing someone for a skill you don't think they have has various downfalls:

   a. You are being phony.

   b. Skills are often randomly placed there by a LinkedIn algorithm and the person may not even want to be endorsed for them.

   c. You signal to that person that you really don't know them well.

5. We recommend <u>only doing one endorsement for the same person every few days</u>. This helps you stay top of mind for a longer period of time rather than endorsing the same individual for multiple skills at once. Remember the goal is to play the long game, so it's better to sprinkle ten endorsements over four weeks than ten endorsements for the same person in one day.

> **+👤 PRO TIP:** Don't use the endorsement box at the top. Instead, scroll down to the list of skills for this person towards the bottom of the page. This list defaults from highest to lowest (what other people are selecting for skills). However, the user can also arrange this list to their liking (see our tip on managing endorsements). Always start by endorsing individuals for the skill you know they have that is highest on this list. Avoid the endorsement box at the top, mainly because LinkedIn generates the skills in this box. The skills listed further down the page in the list format are more credible.

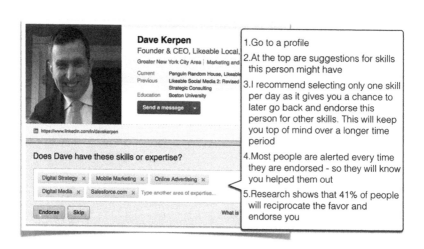

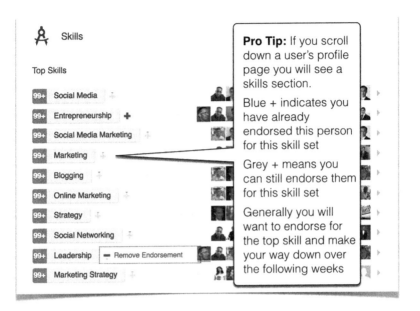

14 WRITING RECOMMENDATIONS

WHY

A boss, colleague or employee may have positively influenced your career. They may have inspired you to post-it-forward (see Tip #11) or they may have asked you for a recommendation (see Tip #15). Writing recommendations helps improve the recipient's credibility and creates goodwill for the recommender and receiver. Additionally, the person is likely to return the favor and write a recommendation for you.

> **"** Ninety-one percent of customers say they'd give referrals.
> Only 11% of salespeople ask for referrals. **"**
> —Dale Carnegie

Not only does it look good for the recipient, but it also reflects positively upon your giving attitude and team mindset. Moreover, your name will appear next to your recommendation—think of it as free advertising that your prospects might see.

HOW

Writing a LinkedIn recommendation may sound difficult, but it can be done in four simple steps. The guidance below will assist you in writing winning recommendations.[26]

1. **Set the stage of your relationship with the person:** Give a simple summary of the relationship between you and the person whom you are writing a recommendation for. This will give the reader the benefit of context.

2. **Talk about the position you were in when you worked with them:** Did you and the person you are writing a recommendation for work together in the same role or perhaps multiple roles? No matter the position, explain parts of the job they exceled in and tasks they were held responsible for. This gives the reader a summary of what they did in certain roles.

3. **Share results:** Results can be shown by a short success story or metrics. Sharing results gives the reader a real example of what the person is capable of and can leave a great impression. Connect these achievements with the individual's qualities.

4. **Tell a personal note:** End with a personal note of your hopes for them or a personal reflection of your experience working with the individual.

> **+ PRO TIP:** Be concise. Sum up the person's main responsibilities and characteristics, avoiding inconsequential tasks or roles. Keep in mind that LinkedIn gives a 3,000-character limit when it comes to recommendations.[27]

15 REQUESTING RECOMMENDATIONS

WHY

93% of purchase decisions are influenced by social media recommendations.[28] Recommendations matter—especially on LinkedIn. High-quality recommendations boost your digital reputation and are searchable, allowing prospects to easily find out what others are saying about you. Start thinking of yourself and your recommendations as a searchable product.

HOW

1. To access the recommendation page ⇨ view your profile ⇨ click the drop down arrow right next to the blue "view profile" button to see the "Ask to be recommended" link. I strongly recommend you contact (email, text, face-to-face) the person you are requesting a recommendation from prior to sending the recommendation request. Asking face-to-face is a nice courtesy and will increase your success rate of receiving the recommendation.

2. Another option is to go to www.linkedin.com/recs/ask.

3. Choose Wisely—Request recommendations from people who are able to validate your work ethic with detail and provide unique descriptions. Select three to five people from past jobs and volunteer experiences who you think will be able to highlight your different talents and industry background. Each recommendation should say something different, which accentuates on a variety of your skill sets.

4. Avoid using LinkedIn's default subject heading of "Can you recommend me?" Instead, consider personalizing your request by and pointing out how much you value their expertise and highlight the impact they had on you.

5. Write the recommendation yourself. Acknowledge that the recommender may be strapped for time and it'd be convenient if you drafted the recommendation. Let them know they can add, change or delete any of the text to ensure it is a genuine reflection of their tone. See Tip #14 on how to write a good recommendation.

6. Send a thank you note (both online and offline) immediately once you receive their recommendation!

16 FACE-2-FACE CANNOT BE REPLACED

93% of communication is non-verbal.[29] If you are spending all your time communicating via a screen, you are doing yourself a tremendous disservice. Great sales people understand building relationships that lead to success require a balance between online and offline communication.[30]

- Research indicates people are twice as likely to remember you if you shake hands, and also shows that they will respond in a friendlier and more open manner.[31]

- 88% of people believe others are less polite on social media than in person.[32]

- Our tone in digital messages is misinterpreted 50% of the time.[33]

- Developing your network requires online <u>and</u> offline interaction. Digital tools are powerful and should be used to augment your interaction when time and distance are an issue. Keep in mind that face-to-face cannot be replaced.

LEARNING MOMENT

• •

Shorthand writing, abbreviations, Internet slang and emoticons can quickly distort the intended meaning of your messaging. Below is a text from a Mom asking one of her two daughters for help interpreting a message.[34]

17 | STATUS UPDATES THAT GET NOTICED

WHY

Sharing status updates with your connections is a great way to provide valuable content to readers, engage customers and draw attention to your profile. All of which are factors that can generate leads. Quick Sprout reports that posting 20 status updates a month will help reach 60% of your unique audience monthly.[35] A larger audience will lead to more opportunities for sales.

HOW

According to LinkedIn, informative updates receive the highest engagement rate. If providing valuable content were easy, everyone would be doing it. Below are 4 techniques to provide informative and helpful status updates that are impactful:

1. Post industry insights. Posting trends, research-backed predictions and observations and facts affecting the business landscape will position you as an expert within your field. 60% of users value these industry insights.[36]

2. Share company news. Keeping potential clients in the know with what your company is doing can help build trust. 53% of users are interested in company news.[37]

3. Encourage audience participation. Ask relevant questions and encourage people's comments and opinions. Example: Who do you think will reach Mars first: Elon Musk, Richard Branson or Jeff Bezos?

4. Include a form of media. Photos and videos attract viewers and allow for a 98% higher comment rate than a post of just text.[38]

+ PRO TIP: Know when to post. According to HubSpot, the best times to post are Tuesday, Wednesday and Thursday during business hours. The most clicks and shares occur Tuesdays between 10 a.m. and 11 a.m.[39]

Everyone is winning when you are providing valuable content. Share status updates you would like to see and that are a good representation of your company.

LEARNING MOMENT

• •

OPPORTUNITY: Rebecca Mayne started a new career as a yoga instructor and needed to quickly develop a paying client base. She soon discovered it was difficult to differentiate herself from the thousands of other yoga instructors—she was struggling to sell her classes.

ACTION: Rebecca turned to LinkedIn to promote her experience, credentials and continuously updated her yoga schedule via status updates.

RESULT: Rebecca started to gain a steady following on LinkedIn with potential students and studio owners. Through these new connections, she started getting hired by students to come to their businesses and workplaces to conduct private sessions.[40]

18 | MANAGING YOUR ENDORSEMENTS

WHY

Endorsements reinforce trust—similar to the comfort you feel when reading a five-star review on a product you are about to purchase.

HOW

1. Go to your profile and scroll down to "Skills & Endorsements."

2. Click the +Add Skill link which is above and to the right of your skills.

3. Type in the relevant skills that represent what you do best.

4. To manage endorsements, click the "Manage Endorsements" link. This is very helpful in that it allows you to arrange and order your endorsements for viewers. If you want "Strategic Thinking" listed higher than "Public Speaking," you can move it up or down your ranking list. Or, if you want to decline endorsements for certain skills, you can do so here.

5. Focus on those areas of expertise that best represent you and select a list of skills that easily portray a story of who you are.

> ❝ Associate yourself with people of good quality, for it is better to be alone than in bad company. ❞
> —Booker T. Washington

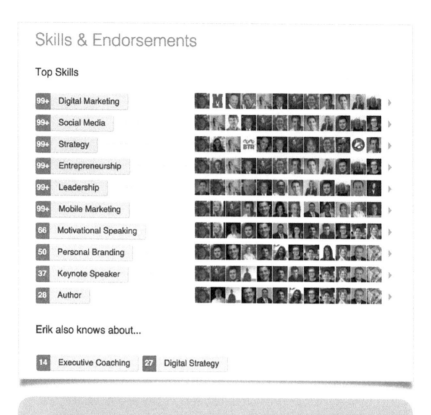

> **+👤 PRO TIP:** The easiest way to get endorsements is to endorse other people you have interacted with, respect and can vouch for their work. Upon receiving your endorsement, they will often return the favor by endorsing you.

Keep your endorsements to a set of 10-15 skills. This will keep your profile very clean and focused. If you have 50 different endorsements, it's analogous to being a "Jack of all trades, master of none."

If someone endorses you for a skill that doesn't fit you, simply decline the endorsement. You can decline endorsements when alerted about them by clicking on the "x" button near the endorsement. Or, at any time, you can go to the edit section of your endorsements and delete all the endorsements for a certain category (e.g., Executive Coaching, Training, etc.).

LEARNING MOMENT

• •

CHALLENGE: Mitchell Levy struggled with getting views on his LinkedIn profile.

ACTION: Instead of treating his profile as a resume, he decided to treat his profile as a SEO-optimized landing page. Previously, Mitchell had ignored the skill endorsements he received on LinkedIn. To help drive traffic to his profile, Mitchell decided that skill endorsements might speak the loudest to viewers of his profile. With this mindset, he sent out emails to his network requesting them to endorse his skills on LinkedIn.

RESULTS: After sending out his emails, his skill endorsements soared from 10-20 endorsements per skill to 99+ endorsements per skill.[41]

TAGGING PEOPLE

WHY

Tagging on LinkedIn is one of the best ways to segment and manage your network.

HOW

Similar to Facebook, LinkedIn allows you to create "tags" that you can attach to your connections. Later you can sort your connections through that tag. This allows you to keep up with and stay in touch with your key prospects by sharing the occasional Pulse article (or your own post).

For example, if one of my key prospects is a marketer who targets Medical Professionals, all I have to do is:

1. Create a Tag called Medical Marketing Consultant (they can't see it).

2. Do an advanced search on the keywords;
    Marketing OR Marketer OR Consultant AND medical.

3. Sort by 1st level connections.

4. Open and tag each connection with the Medical Marketing Consultants tag.

5. Open connection.

6. Filter by tag / tag name.

7. Hover over the prospect and send a message.

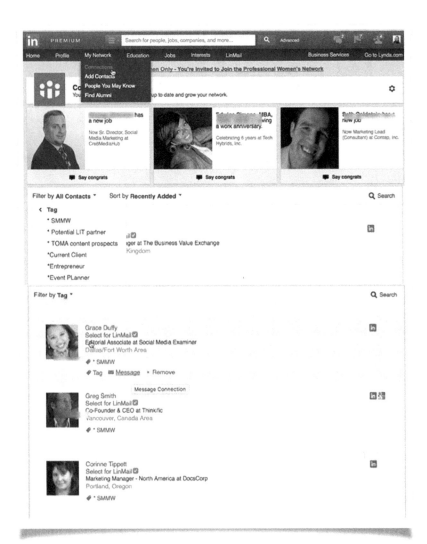

+👤 PRO TIP: I might lead with, "As a medical marketing consultant, are you frustrated with LinkedIn's new visibility limitations?" And then in the body of the message, I would resolve their particular point of pain by sharing an article I wrote or found that they would find interesting.

You can even have your assistant create and assign tags for you. And then (after you go through and check the lists) have them send the messages to the tagged individuals. I also recommend creating an editorial calendar to keep track of what you sent to whom.

Of course you can do this for as many different tagged groups as you want. Often sharing the same tip, just using a different subject line.

I don't have to be the creator of the content I share. I just need to share it. I'm also not going to try and sell them my own product or service (yet). I'm just trying to create a feeling of trust and top of mind awareness, so that when they need me (or hear of someone who needs a LinkedIn consultant), they will think of me! And then of course, once I have established that trust and awareness, I might occasionally send them my latest product or offer, although always wrapped in a blanket of warm fuzzy usefulness.

A big thanks to Viveka von Rosen for supplying this tip. Please check out her outstanding insights around LinkedIn including her books *LinkedIn Marketing: An Hour A Day* and *LinkedIn Security: Who's Watching You?*

20 POSTING SHAREABLE CONTENT

WHY

Consistently posting content helps position you as a thought leader and provides valuable insights and information to your clients, prospects and partners. Research is an integral part of the buy cycle, with the average consumer viewing more than 11.4 pieces of content prior to making a purchase.[42]

HOW

1. **Go to the home page** on your LinkedIn account (First page that will pop up when you log in).

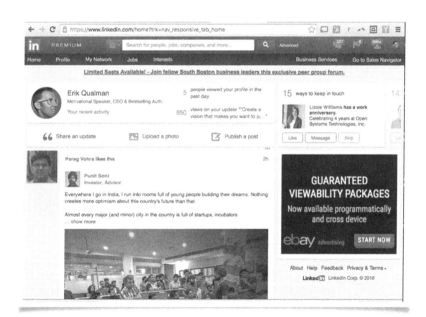

2. **Understand your options**: You can share an update, upload a photo or publish a post. You want to reach as many people as you can with your posts; note that LinkedIn's busiest times are morning to midday during the week.[43]

3. **Ask yourself**, "What am I hoping to achieve?" Are you trying to bring individuals to your LinkedIn page? Increase awareness for your company? Are you interested in search engine optimization (SEO—Showing near the top in Google) traction? Know what your objectives are and develop a content plan to meet these objectives.

4. **Ensure updates are relevant** to your connections. What's happening within your company or industry right now? Post compelling content that is relevant and shareable to your consumers.

5. **Have call to action** with each post, include a compelling image, engage consumers with questions and do this on a consistent and frequent basis.

6. **Share the love!** Share industry news, thought leader content and other relevant stories so it's not "all about you." Selecting other insightful articles and summarizing the content for your readers is just as important as writing original content.

+& PRO TIPS

- According to LinkedIn, a company's updates that include links can have up to 45% higher follower engagement than updates without links.[44]

+👤 MORE PRO TIPS (continued)

- Social Media Management Software like Hootsuite, Sprin-klr, Spredfast, etc. makes it easy to manage your updates.

- Longer posts, those over 800 words, seem to perform well on LinkedIn.

- Use images whenever possible. On average, pages with images or videos draw 94% more views.[45]

  - Visuals are processed 60,000x faster than text.[46]

  - 90% of information transferred to the brain is visual.[47]

  - 65% of the entire population are visual learners.[48]

- Many companies use Showcase Pages on LinkedIn, which allow you to create distinct platforms for the various aspects of your business, each with its own messaging to share with a target audience.

According to LinkedIn, the 5 steps to engaging followers are:

1. Establish your presence

2. Attract followers

3. Engage followers

4. Amplify through the network

5. Analyze and refine

Consistently posting value-added content will increase your credibility as a reliable source on LinkedIn; your post could be featured in the main LinkedIn newsfeed, which can result in millions of views.

There is a lot of confusion between Pulse, Posts and Publisher. They are all related, but slightly different. Here's a breakdown by Viveka von Rosen:

- Posts are long-form blog-like articles that YOU write on LinkedIn.

- Publisher is the feature where you write and share YOUR posts.

- Pulse is the newsreader where Influencer and some member's posts can be seen and read.

IMPROVING TEAM SATISFACTION

• •

CHALLENGE: John inherited a team whose satisfaction levels were at an all-time low of 28%. Moreover, the low moral negatively impacted customer satisfaction, which was also at an all-time low of 24%.

ACTION: John turned to his LinkedIn network for council and advice. What had others done in similar situations?

RESULT: John gathered new ideas to reengage his team: listening, relationship building and recognizing talent. Major projects started getting out the door faster, helping to raise team satisfaction levels to 90%.[49]

21 | EMBEDDING VIDEO

WHY

Videos are a great way to provide additional value to your readers. According to Sprout Social, links to videos that play directly can result in a 75% higher share rate.[50] Embedded videos are when the video shows and is able to play directly within the article/post—meaning the user can stay on the same page. This easier for viewers to forward as well, increasing the possibility of more views and shares. Simply including a link to the video does not give readers the same ease of access to watch, which is why embedding the video is much more effective. How important is video? By 2018, 69 percent of Internet traffic will be video.[51]

HOW

1. Upload or select an existing video from YouTube (Vimeo, etc. but for ease, let's focus on YouTube). In order to obtain the embedded link, the video must be posted to YouTube.

2. Under the YouTube video, click Share ⇨ Embed and copy the link.

3. When publishing your post, click Add Video and paste the embedded link.

4. The video will now appear in your blog post.

+👤 PRO TIP: Consumers are 64% more likely to buy a product after they have watched a video about the product.[52] If your company is promoting a new product or service in a blog post, be sure to embed a video to increase sales.

22 RECRUITING TEAMMATES

WHY

20,000 voices selling your product or service are better than one voice.

Sales in the analog world is a team sport. The same is true when it comes to social selling—arguably more so—since word of mouth is on digital steroids.

Engaging other employees from your company, friends and partners as social selling teammates will dramatically scale your network and voice. It will increase the probability that potential customers will hear about you and your offerings.

Assume you have 10 teammates, each with an average of 200 connections. Instead of simply reaching those 200 connections, you now have expanded your reach to 2,000 via your "Influencer Team."

> " Surround yourself with only people who are going to lift you higher. "
> —Oprah Winfrey

HOW

1. Go to the LinkedIn search bar and type your company name.

2. Refine the search to show only 1st connections—I did this for an amazing company I used to work for called EF Education First and had 171 1st connections.

3. Keep growing your team. Now, have your "antennae" up in the offline world for other possible teammates. If a partner or employee impresses you, ask them to connect on LinkedIn.

4. Share: The next time you are going to send something to a prospect or client, ask yourself if your Influence Team would be interested in it as well. If the answer is yes, be sure to include them, as it will increase your potential reach both online and offline (remember these people still engage in conversations at lunch, over beers, etc.). The more they know, the more you grow.

5. Reward: If a teammate was influential in closing a deal—make sure to give credit where credit is due. Depending on their influence and your company policy, offer tickets to a ballgame, a day at the spa or a $10 Starbucks gift card.

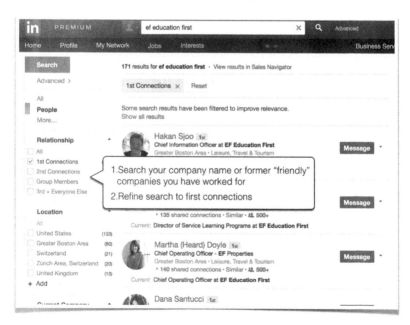

23 PLAYING THE LINKEDIN LONG GAME

WHY

Playing the long game will result in more sales over time.

HOW

As alluded to earlier, if you're at a cocktail party and walked up to four people that were laughing and having a good time, you wouldn't interrupt by saying, "My name is John Jacobs and this is why I'm great and this is what I sell." This type of approach obviously doesn't work in the offline world and the same holds true in the online world.

However, most of us forget this when we are online. Rather than developing relationships, we think every interaction needs to be transactional or black and white. Am I getting a sale today or not? Without first building trust with LinkedIn connections, it will be extremely difficult to sell anything. This makes sense, because the same concept holds true in the offline world—build trust, then sell.

LINKEDIN LONG GAME:

1. Figure out a set of ideal customers—you should have this from your offline activity.

2. Determine what is the most important driver for them—usually by asking a few simple questions (see next page).

3. Deliver helpful information in a relevant and authentic manner.

4. Build a level of trust over time demonstrating that you are reliable and have your customer's best interest in mind, even if it entails recommending a product or solution other than the one you are selling. The customer may not purchase from you the first time around, but they might place orders in the future from you if you develop this trust. Remember the old adage, *"Fool me once, shame on you. Fool me twice, shame on me."*

EXAMPLE OUTREACH MESSAGE ON LINKEDIN (TO A CONNECTION)

Wow! What an exciting win for (insert customer's favorite sports team here). Aside from this win, what is (customer's company) working on nowadays that has you most excited? What's the biggest hurdle that might prevent this initiative from reaching its full potential?

Is there anything I can send or do that might help?

Best, Erik

Notice the opening sentence makes the message personal. It certainly doesn't need to be sports related and in fact, can be anything you know may be of interest or a sentence about a relevant current event. The next three sentences are questions about them and ones that most people like to talk about. If the person isn't interested in talking about what has them the most excited, then it's time to move onto the next opportunity.

The question about the biggest hurdle is one they may not even have thought about here; you are adding value by asking a thought-provoking question! Better to hear this question from you first than from their boss. Lastly, as with most conversations you'll need to ask, how can I help? Your offer to help should be specific and provide the option of a tangible deliverable. In this example above, we are asking if we can send anything down the road (remember we are playing the long game). You might ask something more precise like, "Would it help if I sent over a few case studies of customers that are facing very similar challenges and what they did to resolve it?"

24 SPAMMERS NEVER PROSPER

WHY

Do you like spam? No. So why would you send spam? Don't.

HOW

Now that we have armed you with the amazing tool, LinkedIn, think of it as the world's first hammer—the worst thing you can do is believe that everything is a nail. As you have seen, most of this book is about *Dos*, but here are a few *Don'ts*.

Content and communication only become spam when it is of no value to the receiver. To avoid spamming your connections, customers and prospects, avoid the following:

1. Don't post marketing messages as status updates—a good rule of thumb is 9 value filled status updates for every 1 update about yourself. Remember the best use of light is always to shine it on others, not yourself.

2. Non-custom requests to people you don't know. Too many people use the default connection request. Unless you know the person well—meaning you are 100% confident they will accept your request, then this is a big no-no. It's best to customize every request. I did a test once and found some people were vehemently upset upon receiving a generic connection request from me.

3. Sending long, unsolicited, sales pitch emails. Don't transfer bad email practices over to LinkedIn—they will get the same result: annoying your potential customers.

4. Posting a sales or self-promotional message inside a group before adding any value to the group. This doesn't work and it tarnishes your name and your company's name.

25 PROTECTING YOUR PRIVACY

WHY

Anyone connected on LinkedIn is able to search and find you. The privacy settings on your account only change how you appear on search engines. A general rule of thumb on what to keep private is to ask yourself, "Would I be okay with everyone knowing this about me or my business?" Studies show that the more a person knows about you via LinkedIn, the more likely they are to buy from you. In fact, 68% of consumers feel more positive about a brand after consuming content from that particular brand.[53]

Whatever your comfort level, I recommend taking the following off your profile:

HOW

1. **Age identifiers:** Including your birthday, years you went to school, etc. Age discrimination persists and you want your qualifications to resonate first. Include your alma mater but avoid listing the year you graduated.

2. **Ethnicity as a description:** Unfortunately, discrimination still occurs.

3. **Religious affiliations**

4. **Reasons for leaving previous job:** This is a topic to be discussed in private and not appropriate for public view.

5. **Specific street addresses:** Remember, LinkedIn is public and for security reasons, you may not want this information available for just anyone.

6. **Phone numbers of previous employers:** This is to protect your previous employer's privacy.

7. **Salary figures**

26 | PRIVACY TOOLS

WHY

Unlike many other social networks, LinkedIn shows who has viewed your profile and alerts others when you have viewed their profile. How people view your profile is determined by the profile settings you select, so it's important to know and understand your settings.

LinkedIn also gives you the power to choose how your profile appears in search engines, who sees your connections, how you rank, whether you want the option of 'viewers who viewed this profile also viewed' to show, if your profile changes are shared with your network and the option to notify connections when you're in the news. Phew. Don't worry, it's pretty easy.

Bottom line, it's important to know and take control of how others see you on LinkedIn.

HOW

Click on your profile image: Go to Privacy & Settings ⇨ Manage ⇨ Profile Privacy to choose your settings. Here, you will be given the option to update what people see when they view your profile. Clicking on each option explains what it does and how to change it, thus making it easy to manage your profile privacy.

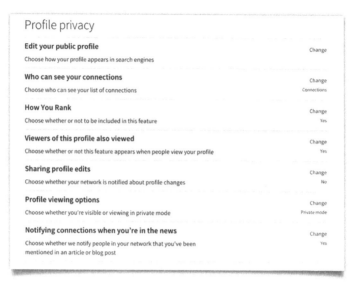

How you choose to appear to others dictates whether or not you can see who has viewed your profile. For example, if you choose to be anonymous when viewing profiles, you will not have the capability to see who has viewed your profile. There are three options for how to appear to others:

1. Name and Current Title with your Profile Picture

2. Anonymous with your industry and title

3. Invisible to other users

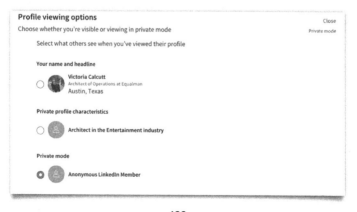

ACTION ITEM

Be positive about what you want others to see on your profile and check your privacy settings regularly.

+ PRO TIP: As you will see throughout this book, trust and transparency are good for business. Many studies have shown that by viewing a prospects' LinkedIn profile, you have a greater chance to book a meeting, close the sale, etc. This makes sense, they can see you are interested and now they have a name and a face—you are real. In fact, a company called SearchQuant has a tool that will automatically view hundreds of prospects' profiles for you—saving you time and hassle.

If the prospect then views your profile, this becomes a warmer lead. This gets back to human nature—people get interested in you when you show interest in them.

27 | SALES + MARKETING = DEADLY COMBO

WHY

Historically, marketing would tell customers *what* they wanted and sales would tell them *why* they wanted it. Today, readily available information has empowered customers and has shifted the sales game. Having sales and marketing aligned around LinkedIn can prove to be a powerful combination. Lack of alignment between the two can be deadly for the business.

> *❙❙* All it takes is hearing one too many times 'Where are the good leads?' from sales and 'You don't follow-up on everything' from marketing to know there's an opportunity for better alignment. *❙❙*
> —Greg Forrest, Sr. Manager
> Marketing Operations & Demand Center, Concur[54]

As a salesperson, you expect company executives to have sales and marketing teams aligned around similar goals or key performance indicators (KPIs). If you aren't sure, it doesn't hurt to ask and as an individual sales person you should.

HOW

1. Ask marketing what their short and long term plans efforts for LinkedIn are.

2. Ask marketing for suggestions on how you could improve— even if their suggestions don't help in the short term, you will be first on their list if they want to test something with their

marketing dollars and might provide you with bonus exposure on LinkedIn.

3. Stay abreast of marketing's activity on LinkedIn; you never want a client to know more about your business than you do.

4. Ask what premium services marketing is currently paying for on LinkedIn and if there is any way you can leverage these.

CASE STUDY: CONCUR

• •

CONCUR: Provider of integrated travel & expense management solutions

CHALLENGE: Frustrated sales team by perceived poor lead quality; marketing frustrated by perceived lack of follow-up from the sales team on said leads.

ACTION: Concur developed workshops to align process and goals between marketing and sales—specifically making the efforts on LinkedIn more coordinated.

RESULT: 20% year-over-year growth.[55]

---

28 GOING CROSS CHANNEL

WHY

Reaching your customer where they want to be reached when they are ready to buy is critical to increasing sales.

HOW

We have focused on LinkedIn throughout this book; it's the greatest selling and prospecting tool we have ever seen. However, this doesn't mean you replace all your offline and online strategies that have worked in the past. Specifically:

Social selling doesn't replace your coffees, meetings, lunches and golf outings. Refer to Tip #16: Face-2-Face cannot be replaced. The tips and tools in this book are designed to help start and deepen relationships when time and distance are an issue.

Use your EQ (emotional intelligence) to determine when and where each individual customer wants to be reached both offline and online—keeping in mind that everyone differs. If a client loves the ballet, taking them to a football game doesn't make much sense. So use Facebook, email, direct mail, birthday cards and such to properly cross sell and augment your LinkedIn social selling activity.

There is exponential power in meeting people for lunches, as well as having your message appear in your prospect's mailbox, inbox and social feed.

CASE STUDY: MOVIG TARGETS

● ●

SITUATION: Moving Targets, a national direct marketing agency, has discovered the power of cross channel selling first hand.

ACTION: Combined their online advertising buys with their direct marketing mailings.

RESULT: Increased response rates by 25%.

Moving Target's CMO Jenna Gross' advice when combining cross-channel selling with social selling: "Your message should say, 'Here's the outcome we help people like you accomplish.' The star of the show is not you, your company history or the feature of your product/service. Rather, it's the result you deliver consistently to your happy customers."

29 GROUPS

WHY

Build relationships, learn insights and establish thought leadership. 64% of top sellers participate in groups.[56]

You are 70% more likely to get an appointment for an unexpected sale if you join LinkedIn Groups.[57]

HOW

1. Select a group relevant to your industry and one that you are interested in. If you aren't interested in what you sell, your buyers won't be interested either.

2. Listen to get a feel for the tone of comments and conversations—the best social sellers are the best listeners.

3. Try to determine the influencers in the group and which type of posts and comments attract the most attention.

4. Start by liking a few posts or comments—this displays your name and profile photo in prominent locations, helping build your equity in the group.

5. Determine if you can add value or identify a problem that the group has where you might be able to offer a solution.

6. Comment where you can add value—try to mirror the tone and behavior of the top influencers, but in your own voice.

7. Start a new discussion.

8. Turn on the email option so you can be alerted of activity in the group.

9. Dedicate a certain amount of time per week to engage in the group.

> **+👤 PRO TIP:** Go deep on one to two worthwhile groups rather than spreading yourself too thin across three to five groups. Closed groups are often less cluttered with spam since a community manager actively monitors them.

Having trouble finding the right group? Each group has a "group statistics" button you can click on to determine how many users, activity, type of users, etc. each group has. If you find three groups that look worthwhile, you can figure out which one is the best for your prospecting needs by clicking this group statistics button and reviewing the information and statistics listed.[58]

❝ To cultivate kindness is a valuable part of the business of life. ❞
—Samuel Johnson

30 | EXPORT CONTACTS INTO EMAIL

WHY

Let's face it—not everyone is as responsive on LinkedIn as you are. Never fear, there is a secret way to get the email addresses of any of your LinkedIn connections.

HOW

1. Go to: https://www.linkedin.com/people/export-settings.

2. From the drop down, select .csv (good for Gmail, Yahoo, Outlook, etc.) or VCF (Mac OS). Most will use .csv.

3. Hit the export button.

4. Voila, this will download an Excel file with your contacts name and email address

5. You can find the email you are looking for and/or upload it to your Gmail, Yahoo, Outlook, Salesforce, CRM, etc.

> **+👤 PRO TIP:** This is another reason to grow your connections on LinkedIn, as it will help grow your traditional email contact database.

LEARNING MOMENT

• •

CHALLENGE: After a personal move, Megan Garrett, needed to build her client base for her litigation practice in her new region.

ACTION: Megan disliked being "sales-y" at offline networking events, so she often let her LinkedIn profile do the talking for her. At offline events, she wouldn't ask for business cards, she'd simply indicate "I'll connect with you on LinkedIn."

RESULT: She started to build her client roster, slowly, but surely. "My profile really helps me show, not tell, someone that I'm a capable professional."[59]

SECTION 2 · BONUS TIPS AND TRICKS

Some may find this section the most helpful and fun. In this section, we will dive deeper on some of the concepts that have already been presented, as well as give you additional quick tricks and pro tips.

LIVE STREAMING 30-SECOND VIDEOS

At the time of this writing, LinkedIn just announced they would be testing live streaming video with 500 select influencers. If all goes well, they will roll it out to everyone. I strongly encourage you to test a few videos when this capability becomes available. It will not be for everyone, as you need to be comfortable in front of a camera. It is worth testing right away, as some of you will make millions of dollars just by doing this alone.

The key is to be yourself and focus on the niche that you know best. Always ask yourself before turning on the camera how you are going to provide value to the viewer, client or prospect. This can be done via humor, facts, summarizing news, etc. Play to your strengths. If you aren't funny, then don't try and use humor. Test it out as soon as you can, as the first movers on platforms generally attract large numbers of followers.

FIND ANY EMAIL ADDRESS

Some users on LinkedIn require you to know their email to connect with them. This can be frustrating when you have meet someone or know someone and are trying to connect with them on LinkedIn but don't have there email address. The good news is Ginny Soskey, Section Editor of the HubSpot blog, came up with this effective step process to help discover any email: Companies have email structures (e.g., @nike.com, @ford.com, @equalman.com) so our first step is discovering what this is.

Step 1

Where can we find company email structures?

1. Check out LinkedIn. If you find a first connection that works at the company, look at their "Contact Info" section on their profile to see if they included their work email.

2. Press releases are a great place to uncover a company's email address structure. Search for a company's recent announcements with Google or on their website, if they have a PR person, their contact information should be at the bottom of the release.

3. Try the company's blog as well, it will usually include the author's contact information at the bottom or top of the page.

This site can also help: http://emailbreaker.com/

Step 2

Once you have the structure, put in the name. Say your prospect's name is Kelly and she works at Equalman. Here is what her email will look like:

kelly@equalman.com

This isn't always 100% accurate because Kelly can be spelt in multiple ways:

kelli@equalman.com
kellie@equalman.com
kely@equalman.com

Step 3:

You could plug in all the email addresses you think are possible with different spellings. We suggest sending the email message to yourself and putting the different possible email addresses as bcc, this way if one of the emails works the prospect won't see all the variations you tried.

However, there are free tools from HubSpot (HubSpot Sales and HubSpot Sidekick) that can make your life easier. If you download these tools then you can:

Compose a message in Gmail and enter each email into the "To" line. If they're valid, HubSpot Sales will show their profile with information like where they work and their social media profiles.

See how Brian's information appears in his contact profile? We **know** this is a legit email address. On the other hand, if the email isn't valid, we'll get a blank profile and will have to keep guessing. Yes, this is hard work, but hard work is something your sales competition isn't willing to do.

Step 4

Perhaps we guessed wrong at the email structure. Below are the most common structures (source: HubSpot):

Structure	Steve	Stephen	Stephan	Steven
firstname_lastname @company.com	steve_lewis @cc.com	stephen_lewis @cc.com	stephan_lewis @cc.com	steven_lewis @cc.com
firstnameLastname@ company.com	stevelewis @cc.com	stephenlewis @cc.com	stephanlewis @cc.com	stevelewis @cc.com
firstnameinitial_lastn ame@company.com	s_lewis @cc.com	s_lewis @cc.com	s_lewis @cc.com	s_lewis @cc.com
firstnameinitiallastna me@company.com	slewis @cc.com	slewis @cc.com	slewis @cc.com	slewis @cc.com
firstnamelastnameinit ial@company.com	stevel @cc.com	stephenl @cc.com	stephanl @cc.com	stevenl @cc.com
lastname@company. com	lewis @cc.com	lewis @cc.com	lewis @cc.com	lewis @cc.com
firstnameinitialmiddle nameinitiallastname @company.com	steveklewis @cc.com	stephenklewis @cc.com	stephanklewis @cc.com	stevenklewis @cc.com

Hopefully this worked for you so you can start focusing on sending a message that can't be ignored.

SALES NAVIGATOR

WHY

If you can afford some of LinkedIn's selling tools such as Sales Navigator, you can make your life much simpler.

If you cannot afford the cost of the Premium tools, don't fret because you can still do the same tasks manually. However, if you can afford the cost, I highly recommend purchasing them. In the grand scheme of things, they are relatively inexpensive.

Below, I'm going to go over the biggest win with Sales Navigator; however, there are so many things this tool can do—from integrating with Salesforce to recommending leads—that it would require another book. Fortunately, you can go to LinkedIn for tutorials and updates.

HOW

Imagine you sell outdoor billboard space in Michigan. Over time, you've discovered that your sweet spot for selling these boards is to CMOs of mid-sized Michigan-based companies. Using Sales Navigator's Lead generator, you can do the following:

1. Target by zip code: Select the zip code of your hometown—sharing this commonality with prospects can only help your chances of developing a relationship.

2. Target by title: I entered Chief Marketing Officer.

3. Target by company size: I selected 1,001 – 5,000 and 5,001 – 10,000.

These 3 simple steps described on the previous page resulted in 24 viable prospects from my hometown.

PRO TIP: Start with regions and zip codes where you have some tie (you worked there, you lived there, etc.). This familiarity strategy applies across all selectable categories.

I asked someone at LinkedIn, who asked to remain anonymous, what their clients like best about Navigator. This was their response: *"Navigator is so cool for large sales and marketing teams because it has a feature called team link. It reads your current company and links your colleagues network. Impossible to know everyone at Oracle for example—navigator does know—this is huge for relationship selling. Very powerful!"*

SEO TIPS
FOR YOUR LINKEDIN COMPANY PROFILE

WHY

Search Engine Optimization (SEO) doesn't have to be difficult. There are several easy ways to manage a company page to drive engagement, boost traffic and improve your overall search rankings, both online and offline. As the name implies, company pages are essentially the same as a personal profile, just for companies.

Some of you reading this are entrepreneurs that will need to do this yourself, while others are salespeople for large organizations. Those in larger organizations should run this by your LinkedIn or marketing team to ensure these tips are being done. These are all opportunities to send prospects your way.

HOW

1. **Keywords matter.** Utilize the 156-character limit for your company's description by being selective about your service offerings. Enriching your company description with who you are, what you do and relevant keywords will make it easier for Google to figure out what your company LinkedIn page stands for. Use tools such as Google's free Keyword Planner or Trends to learn the top search queries for your industry. Remember that members can find your company page solely by keywords, so start learning what your target audience is searching for, then build a description from there.[60]

2. **Empower Employees to Share.** Encourage your employees to update their work experience to include your company. This creates a clickable version of your company's logo on their page, which makes it easier for their network to find you. Plus, it's free branding! Encourage employees to share company updates through their personal pages and vice versa. Personalization is key and as Econsultancy reports, "Businesses currently personalizing web experiences are experiencing an increase in sales of 19% on average."[61] People like to see the individuals and faces behind the companies.

3. **Utilize Marketing Options.** LinkedIn Showcase pages, embed buttons and media links can increase your SEO results. LinkedIn Showcase pages link to your original company page and can be used to emphasize new products, initiatives, brand extensions and any content augmented for specific audiences.

4. **Targeted Ads.** In 2015, 50% of B2B marketers reported they're more likely to buy from a company they've engaged with on LinkedIn.[62] Test some of the targeted ad options LinkedIn has to offer. These ads allow you to target various items including title, company, location and beyond. Driving traffic to or creating awareness around your company page can lead to more followers and higher rankings for your company page.

LINKING OUT

WHY

Putting relevant personal or company website links in your profile will 1) drive traffic to your product/service/brand 2) help your Google search engine ranking—it's like a healthy scoop of broccoli for Search Engine Optimization.

HOW

You can display as many as three website links on your profile, and they can be added from the "**Edit Profile**" page. To add a website:

1. Move your cursor over *"Profile"* at the top of your homepage and select *"Edit Profile."*

2. Click the *"Contact Info"* box near the bottom right of the profile overview section. The profile overview section has your photo in it.

3. Click the Edit icon next to *"Websites."*

4. Choose the type of website from the dropdown list.

    *   *Note:* If you select *"Other"* from the list, you can type in your own website title.

5. Copy and paste your website address into the *"URL"* field.

6. Click *"Save."*

The websites you add will be displayed in the Contact Info section of your profile. (Source: LinkedIn)

+👤 PRO TIP: If you work for Nike, instead of the display text for the website hyperlink saying "Nike," it's better for Google SEO Juice (i.e., items that help you show up high in Google) to list something more specific, such as "Athletic Shoes" or "Sports Gear." Or say your small business is called Gripago and you sell Security Software, you might have the hyperlink be "Security Software" instead of "Gripago." This way if someone searches for Security Software on LinkedIn or they Google, your profile or company website is more likely to come up.

LISTEN FIRST, SELL LAST (BONUS INFO ON TIP #9)

Listen First, Sell Last is so important that we go into more depth below. What does listening actually mean when it comes to digital?

SCIENCE OF COMPASSION

Selling more begins by changing our mental approach and online actions. Research shows that becoming compassionate to others leads to an increase in creativity, problem-solving skills and our sense of connection to others.[63] Compassionate behavior enables our abilities to persist longer at unfavorable tasks and act as a buffer to stress.[64] When you adopt a compassionate approach, not only will you work smarter, longer and more efficiently, but you're also more likely to pick yourself back up when you're down.

Whether you're trying to reach your monthly sales target or land that strategic account you've been chasing, lose the gimmicks because they're too easily detected online. A compassionate approach means thinking of "we" instead of "I."

CULTIVATE DIGITAL MINDFULNESS

We're familiar with the idea that it takes 21 days to form a habit, so make it daily practice to think of your customers as people rather than revenue sources.[65] The easiest way to do this is by asking questions. Practice digital mindfulness by asking your customers questions and actively listening to their answers.

Apply the practices of empathic thinking and digital mindfulness with every post, comment and online action to ensure your business is sincerely in operation to help others. Most of you reading this are familiar with the concept of ABC, Always Be Closing. Often, when it comes to social selling the best way to close sales is to follow the mantra of ABH, Always Be Helping.

BE OVERLY POLITE

Networking is a two-way street. After requesting or accepting a connection, reach out with a friendly, personalized message. Send a sincere compliment and a reminder of who you are and how you met. Scan their profile to learn mutual interests, groups or even universities to bring up specific talking points in your message.

EXAMPLE

Hi Sara,

This is Michele from the Enterprise Sales Strategies Summit. We met at the "How to Influence People" breakout session and I wanted to stay connected. I see that you live in Austin, TX...so do I! Let's grab coffee sometime—organic coffee of course since this is Austin ☺.

Cheers, Michele

@michele

---

*❝ Be weird. Be random. Be who you are.
Because you never know who would love the person you hide. ❞*
—C.S. Lewis

JOIN YOUR UNIVERSITY GROUP

Join your university's alumni page. Utilize an already built network by joining the alumni page and pages of past groups you participated in during college. Remember, you want to provide quality information and insight into any group you join and any content you post.

in LINKEDIN
SOCIAL SELLING SUCCESS CHECKLIST

by Erik Qualman

OVERALL PRINCIPLE

- ☐ ABH: Always Be Helping
- ☐ Play the long game - listen first

LINKEDIN BASICS

- ☐ 100% complete profile
- ☐ Your Summary: Tell a story - less on what you do and more on why you do it
- ☐ Sharp profile photo
- ☐ Keep your info short, focused - don't be a jack-of-all-trades
- ☐ Compelling Banner Image
- ☐ Constantly revise and update
- ☐ Properly link to your website, product, etc.
- ☐ Make it perfect: check for grammar / spelling
- ☐ Periodically review what's working and not working

DAILY

- ☐ Take 3 minutes to Post-It-Forward
- ☐ Endorse one person per day
- ☐ Share relevant content & use images / video
- ☐ Like someone's post
- ☐ Send 3 connection invites
- ☐ Try to setup a lunch or coffee with your connections

ALL-STARS

- ☐ Develop a voice and curate or post content often
- ☐ Standout by being yourself
- ☐ Build out your endorsements to +99
- ☐ Write recommendations for others & ask for recommendations
- ☐ Export contacts into email

SOCIAL SELLING CIRCLE
by Erik Qualman

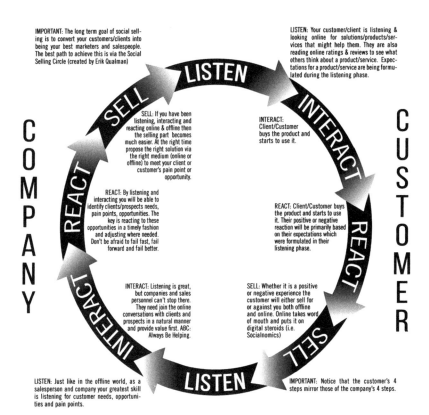

IMPORTANT: The long term goal of social selling is to convert your customers/clients into being your best marketers and salespeople. The best path to achieve this is via the Social Selling Circle (created by Erik Qualman)

LISTEN: Your customer/client is listening & looking online for solutions/products/services that might help them. They are also reading online ratings & reviews to see what others think about a product/service. Expectations for a product/service are being formulated during the listening phase.

SELL: If you have been listening, interacting and reacting online & offline then the selling part becomes much easier. At the right time propose the right solution via the right medium (online or offline) to meet your client or customer's pain point or opportunity.

INTERACT: Client/Customer buys the product and starts to use it.

REACT: By listening and interacting you will be able to identify clients/prospects needs, pain points, opportunities. The key is reacting to these opportunities in a timely fashion and adjusting where needed. Don't be afraid to fail fast, fail forward and fail better.

REACT: Client/Customer buys the product and starts to use it. Their positive or negative reaction will be primarily based on their expectations which were formulated in their listening phase.

INTERACT: Listening is great, but companies and sales personnel can't stop there. They need join the online conversations with clients and prospects in a natural manner and provide value first. ABC: Always Be Helping.

SELL: Whether it is a positive or negative experience the customer will either sell for or against you both offline and online. Online takes word of mouth and puts it on digital steroids (i.e. Socialnomics)

LISTEN: Just like in the offline world, as a salesperson and company your greatest skill is listening for customer needs, opportunities and pain points.

IMPORTANT: Notice that the customer's 4 steps mirror those of the company's 4 steps.

SECTION 3 · FAQS

DOES SOCIAL SELLING REALLY WORK?

A study conducted by Sales for Life of over 45,000 sales reps and 200 companies found that for every $1 invested in social selling, the Return on Investment (ROI) is $5.[66]

An Aberdeen Group study on social selling found that quota attainment, renewal rate and forecast accuracy were better when all sales reps used social media. [67]

WHAT'S THE MAIN PURPOSE OF BEING ON LINKEDIN?

As a sales professional, you need to realize that LinkedIn is not your resume, it's your reputation. There is nothing more important than your reputation when it comes to selling. And in today's world, your online reputation is the first place potential prospects look to determine factors like trust, likeability and reliability. Don't miss out on opportunities—become a LinkedIn rock star today.

WHAT ARE THE TWO MOST CRITICAL ITEMS FOR LINKEDIN SOCIAL SELLING?

1. Ensure how you represent yourself (e.g., profile photo, summary) on LinkedIn honestly showcases who you are and your specific talents and skills. Take the effort to update this often and make certain it's 100% complete.

2. Be Human. The easiest way to achieve this is to put yourself in the shoes of your connections, prospects and clients. Simply

ask yourself before reaching out—how can I help this person today? Make a habit of networking before you need the network and remember to shine the light on others (i.e., Tip #11 Post-It-Forward).

WHAT ARE SOME OF THE TOP MISTAKES YOU SEE SALES PEOPLE MAKE WHEN IT COMES TO SOCIAL SELLING ON LINKEDIN?

1. Being afraid to start.

2. Giving up too fast—remember that relationships take time.

3. Viewing every relationship as a transaction rather than a friendship. Speaking and acting differently than you would offline.

4. Not being consistent. You need to carve out a few minutes per day—start with a few minutes and do this every day. Start small and go from there.

5. Not being responsive enough. When someone asks you a question or for something, make this a top priority. This gets back to consistently checking LinkedIn every day—especially your messages.

6. Not leveraging existing offline connections enough to develop new online connections.

7. Taking old school tactics and trying to use them in new school arenas like LinkedIn.

8. Sending impersonalized requests.

HOW WILL I KNOW IF THE CONTENT THAT I'M POSTING IS WORKING?

Use the "Who's Viewed Your Updates" section located at the top of your homepage. By clicking on this you can see *views*, *likes* and *comments* for your posts. You should track this to see what is and what is not working with your posts and adjust accordingly.

IS IT WORTH BUYING INMAILS? OTHER PREMIUM SERVICES?

We've touched on this question throughout the book. As you may have noticed, I'm a big fan of being as organic and human as possible. My goal isn't to sell; my goal is to provide value (ABH: Always Be Helping). InMail can be highly effective, as well as other premium services from LinkedIn. A good game plan is to exhaust every free/organic avenue as possible and then start to add on premium services as needed. If your company is already buying some premium services, I still recommend starting with the free/organic path first but then quickly complementing this with the premium services that your company is generously sponsoring.

HOW DO I MEASURE THE EFFECTIVENESS OF MY SOCIAL SELLING ON LINKEDIN?

There are many ways to measure your success, but the ultimate success will be more sales. Items to measure that will help you get to more sales are:

1. Increasing your tribe in terms of connections on LinkedIn and how many people are liking or commenting on your status updates and posts.

2. Improving your Social Selling Index (SSI) score.

3. The amount of recommendations and endorsements you receive.

129

4. How many offline meetings you are scheduling as a result of your LinkedIn connections and correspondence.

5. Number of new prospects or leads discovered on LinkedIn.

6. Number of sales that were a direct result of your social selling efforts or influenced by them.

HOW CAN I IMPROVE MY SOCIAL SELLING INDEX (SSI) SCORE?

While there is controversy over how the SSI is derived and its relative importance, I have personally seen a correlation between an increase in my SSI score and my sale effectiveness on LinkedIn. Here's what seems to help the score; even if it doesn't increase your SSI score, these are good things to implement, as they are best practice:

1. Complete your profile 100%. (Tip #2)

2. Have a high resolution profile picture and background banner. (Tip #3)

3. Explain why you do something and how it helps others; avoid the mistake of simply posting what you do. Remember we are building a trusted reputation rather than simply a resume. (Tip #5)

4. Establish meaningful connections. (Tip #10)

5. Network before you need the network. (Tip #11)

6. Search and find prospects. (Tip #7)

7. Post status updates and original content. (Tip #17 & Tip #20)

8. Curate and share other people's content that's relevant for your audience.

9.   Share company content and updates. (Tip #27)

10. Like and comment on other people's content. (Tip #11)

11. If you meet someone offline, try to establish a connection on LinkedIn.

Over the course of writing this book, my score went from 62 to 85 simply by doing the items I list above. Most importantly, my sales are increasing as a result of implementing these best practices.

WILL THE IMPORTANCE OF SELLING ON LINKEDIN CONTINUE TO INCREASE AS MORE AND MORE MILLENNIALS AND CENTENNIALS BECOME BUYERS?

Yes. A study by Google and Millward Brown Digital found that 46% of decision makers are now aged between 18 and 34 years old, which coincidentally, is the largest social media user demographic. This same study forecasts for this trend to continue.[68]

SECTION 4 — BONUS CASE STUDIES

Creating Thought Leaders = Sales

• •

CHALLENGE: National Bank of Canada (NBC), the sixth largest commercial bank in Canada, struggled with the ability to differentiate their wholesale business.

ACTIONS: NBC used LinkedIn to position their wholesalers as "thought leaders" to reach new investment advisors.

RESULTS: NBC experienced a 400% return on investment in the first 10 months, while simultaneously holding 250 meetings with investment advisors within a 3-month period. By using the social media platform, NBC became an innovative leader in the financial service industry, while also positioning NBC wholesalers as in demand experts.[69]

Building Interest for a Non-Profit

• •

CHALLENGE: Meg Harris struggled to find amenities and resources that would allow her daughter, whom suffers from a neurological disease, to travel the world without restrictions.

ACTION: She started a business called SpecialGlobe—essentially a TripAdvisor for special needs families. Meg set out to build her brand by using LinkedIn to network with powerful figures within the travel industry.

RESULT: LinkedIn helped Meg gain connections with a founding member of the Priceline team, as well as other key influencers within the travel industry. Not only did she gain connections through LinkedIn, Meg also gained media attention to help highlight and create awareness for her cause, including USA Today and The Huffington Post.[70]

Sales Team Increases Efficiency
by Ranking Contacts

CHALLENGES: Apptio, a provider of SaaS-based technology business management solutions, found it difficult to classify roles and responsibilities of their LinkedIn contacts.

ACTIONS: Sales reps took time to rank all their LinkedIn contacts by their role and responsibilities to the company.

RESULTS: By ranking their contacts, the sales team became 30-40% more efficient using this social selling approach. The sales team also felt they built a higher level of trust with their stakeholders.[71]

Training Company Closes Sales in 5 Days

• •

CHALLENGE: New Horizons, an independent IT training company, realized their sales team was not utilizing social media to its full potential to find new prospects and push their business forward.

ACTIONS: New Horizons used LinkedIn as a way to build their social media existence, making their social cycle more efficient, gaining new leads and overall gaining more business.

RESULTS: With LinkedIn, the sales team was able to close a $25K deal in just 5 days after contacting the new prospect. The sales team increased their ability to follow the same trend line, as well as other LinkedIn searches. They also increased their number of contacts, thus leading to more opportunities. [72]

HP Gains 300,000 Followers in 2 Months

CHALLENGE: HP, a provider of printers and specialized electronic devices, wanted to make customers more aware of new brand messages and to be able to customize the content of messages for different audiences. They also felt the need to extend their engagement with key IT decision makers.

ACTION: HP used LinkedIn to bring their "Make It Matter" campaign to life via a LinkedIn Follower Ad campaign targeting 15 important markets.

RESULT: LinkedIn helped HP gain 300,000+ followers within 2 months, with an increase of 112% in chief executive followers. HP's followers were also 2.5x more likely to endorse HP solutions than others.[73]

LinkedIn Drinks Its Own Champagne

• •

CHALLENGE: LinkedIn needed to alert members of LinkedIn's Premium solutions and increase its number of subscribers.

ACTION: LinkedIn used its InMail product to promote their Premium Solutions by targeting certain audiences who already used different LinkedIn features, such as Business Plus and Job Seeker.

RESULT: LinkedIn reached out to over 2 million prospects every week, causing a 75% increase in open rates and 800% expansion in conversion rates when using InMail versus using traditional emails.[74]

Investment Banking Services Increase New Investor Sign-Ups 1,205%

• •

CHALLENGE: Seed Equity is a broker dealer specializing in providing investment banking services to startup companies who need to get the word out about investment opportunities to key audiences.

ACTION: Using LinkedIn Spotlight Ads and Promoted Posts, they targeted existing members with investment skills, as well as targeting venture capital and private equity groups within LinkedIn to reach the correct investors.

RESULT: Seed Equity experienced a 1,205% increase of new investors signing up and a 43% growth in followers on their LinkedIn company page. Finally, they were able to extend their reach to 33 new countries.[75]

Consultant Uses Groups
to Gain More Business Deals

● ●

CHALLENGE: Neal Schaffer, a social media business consultant, needed a way to stay ahead of the game in the world of social media.

ACTION: To get the inside scoop on news concerning social media, he turned to LinkedIn groups concerning social media.

RESULT: In these groups, he could interact with others in his field of work, develop new relationships and participate in engaging conversation on hot topics. His connections through these groups have lead him to key networking connections, which have led to him gaining new business deals.[76]

SECTION 5 ACKNOWLEDGMENTS

It takes a village to raise a book. The baby you have in your hands is the result of the tireless effort and contributions from this amazing team:

Jessie Bowers: Cover & interior design

Victoria Calcutt: Contributing author, copyeditor

Marissa Fornaro: Contributing author

Caitlin Higgason: Cover & interior design

Ana Maria Lozano: Producer

Kayla Paschall: Contributing author, research & data, copyeditor

Tracy Yager: Contributing author, copyeditor, attributions

Special thanks to LinkedIn Expert Viveka von Rosen for her guidance and noted contributions in the book—be sure to check out her books!

ABOUT THE AUTHOR: ERIK QUALMAN

Erik Qualman is a #1 Bestselling Author and Motivational Speaker that has performed for sold-out audiences in 45 countries. He is a Pulitzer Prize nominated author that has entertained over 30 million people with his books, blogs, videos and performances.

His *Socialnomics* work has been featured on 60 Minutes to the Wall Street Journal and used by the National Guard and NASA. His book *Digital Leader* propelled him to be voted the 2nd Most Likeable Author in the World behind Harry Potter's J.K. Rowling.

Socialnomics was a finalist for the American Marketing Association's "Book of the Year." Qualman wrote and produced the world's most watched social media video "Social Media Revolution."

Qualman was Academic All-Big Ten in basketball at Michigan State University and has been honored as the *Michigan State University Alum of the Year*. He also has an MBA from the McCombs School of Business and an honorary doctorate from Lake Superior State University. Most importantly, he is still trying to live up to the "World's Best Dad" coffee mug he received from his two daughters.

ADDITIONAL BOOKS & RESOURCES BY ERIK QUALMAN

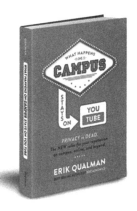

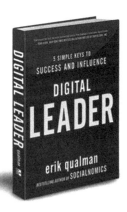

EQUALMAN.COM

SOCIALNOMICS.COM

ENDNOTES

1. LinkedIn. "LinkedIn Social Selling Index." Social Selling Index. Accessed June 27, 2016. https://business.linkedin.com/sales-solutions/the-social-selling-index

2. Deanna Lazzaroni, "60 B2B Marketing Quotes, Stats, and Facts for the Modern Marketer," May 13, 2015, https://business.linkedin.com/marketing-solutions/blog/6/60-b2b-marketing-quotes-stats-and-facts-for-the-modern-marketer#!

3. LinkedIn. "How-To Guide for Social Selling." LinkedIn. Accessed July 18, 2016, https://business.linkedin.com/content/dam/business/sales-solutions/global/en_US/site/pdf/ebooks/how-to-guide-to-social-selling-ebook.pdf

4. http://www.b2bmarketingzone.com/average/benchmark/forrester/

5. LinkedIn. "LinkedIn Social Selling Index." Social Selling Index. 2016. Accessed June 29, 2016. https://business.linkedin.com/sales-solutions/the-social-selling-index

6. Consumer. "Newswire ." Global Advertising Consumers Trust Real Friends and Virtual Strangers the Most. July 7, 2009. Accessed June 27, 2016. http://www.nielsen.com/us/en/insights/news/2009/global-advertising-consumers-trust-real-friends-and-virtual-strangers-the-most.html

7. Arruda, William. "The Easy Way To Get To 500 In LinkedIn." Forbes. April 12, 2015. Accessed June 27, 2016. http://www.forbes.com/sites/williamarruda/2015/04/12/the-easy-way-to-get-to-500-in-linkedin

8. Wallace, Mark. "Breaking Down the Anatomy of a Successful LinkedIn Profile." AkkenCloud. January 08, 2016. Accessed June 27, 2016. http://www.akkencloud.com/breaking-down-the-anatomy-of-a-successful-linkedin-profile/

9. LinkedIn. "Top 10 Actionable Sales Tips." Top 10 Sales Tips and Tricks. Accessed June 27, 2016. https://business.linkedin.com/sales-solutions/social-selling/top-10-sales-tips-tricks?u=0

10. Dave Howe, "The Social Selling FAQs Series: The Ideal LinkedIn Profile," *The Social Selling FAQ Series*, November 2014, https://www.linkedin.com/pulse/20141112132607-87051889-the-social-selling-faqs-series-the-ideal-linkedin-profile

11. LinkedIn. "LinkedIn Help." Showing or Hiding Activity Updates About You. May 2016. Accessed June 27, 2016. https://www.linkedin.com/help/linkedin/answer/78/showing-or-hiding-activity-updates-about-you?lang=en.

12. Jeff Haden. "Stop Using These 16 Terms to Describe Yourself," *LinkedIn,* January, 2013, https://www.linkedin.com/pulse/20130117141235-20017018-stop-using-these-16-terms-to-describe-yourself?trk=mp-details-rc

13. LinkedIn. "SBI's 7th Annual Research Project." LinkedIn SBI Sales Research Report. 2013. Accessed June 29, 2016. https://business.linkedin.com/content/dam/business/sales-solutions/global/en_US/c/pdfs/linkedin sbi-sales-research-report-us-en-130920.pdf

14. Bill Carmody, "4 Ways to Boost Your Social Selling Profile (Courtesy of LinkedIn)," *Inc.com*, Accessed August 5, 2016, http://www.inc.com/bill-carmody/the-4-secrets-of-social-selling-revealed-by-linkedin-s-vp-of-sales-solutions.html

15. Brudner, Emma. "7 Little-Known Ways to Find New Prospects on LinkedIn." September 28, 2015. Accessed May 15, 2016. http://blog.hubspot.com/sales/little-known-ways-to-find-new-prospects-on-linkedin#sm.0000q448lta3pfb8yux2ctvs3pu2u

16. Doerr, John. "6 Keys to Prospecting Success." Rain Group//Blog. Accessed July 22, 2016. http://www.rainsalestraining.com/blog/sales-prospecting-6-keys-to-success

17. Braton, Anna. "Ten Tips For Using Linkedin For Sales Prospecting." Salesforce UK Blog. December 3, 2015. Accessed May 11, 2016. https://www.salesforce.com/uk/blog/2015/12/ten-tips-for-using-linkedin-for-sales-prospecting.html

18. Attach. "Can I Use Attach to See Who Engages with My LinkedIn InMails? - Attach." Attach. Accessed June 27, 2016. https://attach.io/blog/help-center/how-do-i-use-attach-in-linkedin-to-see-who-engages-with-my-inmails/

19. Barbara Giamanco and Kent Gregoire. "Tweet Me, Friend Me, Make Me Buy," HBR.org, July-August 2012 issue, https://business.linkedin.com/sales-solutions/blog/sales-reps/2016/05/revitalizing-the-cold-call

20. http://dswa.org/networking-communication/cold-calls/

21. Experian. "2013 Email Market Study." 2013 Email Market Study. December 2013. Accessed June 29, 2016. http://www.experian.com/assets/marketing-services/white-papers/ccm-email-study-2013.pdf

22. LinkedIn. "Sales Navigator Shortens Sales Cycle & Opens Doors to New Leads." LinkedIn Sales Solutions. 2013. Accessed May 20, 2016. https://business.linkedin.com/content/dam/business/sales-solutions/global/en_US/site/pdf/cs/linkedin-first-business-bank-case-study-en-us.pdf

23. Fowler James H, Christakis Nicholas A. Dynamic spread of happiness in a large social network: longitudinal analysis over 20 years in the Framingham Heart Study BMJ 2008; 337 :a2338

24. "Pay It Forward." Psychology Today. Accessed June 30, 2016. http://www.psychologytoday.com/articles/200607/pay-it-forward

25. Pay It Forward." Psychology Today. Accessed June 30, 2016. http://www.psychologytoday.com/articles/200607/pay-it-forward

26. Wainwright, Corey. "A Simple Formula for a Stellar LinkedIn Recommendation [Quick Tip]." A Simple Formula for a Stellar LinkedIn Recommendation [Quick Tip]. September 30, 2014. Accessed June 01, 2016. http://blog.hubspot.com/marketing/write-linkedin-recommendation#sm.0013u49p4aksfou11l22r5uqbznj5

27. How to Write Good LinkedIn Recommendations. For Dummies. Accessed June 01, 2016. http://www.dummies.com/social-media/linkedin/how-to-write-good-linkedin-recommendations/

28. "Insight Report: Social Media Now Equals TV Advertising in Influence Power on Consumption Decisions." CivicScience. June 8, 2015. Accessed June 30, 2016. https://civicscience.com/ourinsights/insightreports/social-media-equals-tv-advertising-in-influence-power-on-consumption-decisions/

29. "Albert Mehrabian." Wikipedia. June 13, 2016. Accessed June 20, 2016. https://en.wikipedia.org/wiki/Albert_Mehrabian

30. LinkedIn. "The Sophisticated Guide to Marketing on LinkedIn." Sophisticated Guide for Marketing. 2016. Accessed June 28, 2016. https://business.linkedin.com/marketing-solutions/c/14/1/sophisticated-guide-for-marketing

31. Carol Kinsey Goman, "10 Simple and Powerful Body Language Tips for 2012," *Forbes*, January 3, 2012, via a study on handshakes by the Income Center for Trade Shows, http://www.forbes.com/sites/carolkinseygoman/2012/01/03/10-simple-and-powerful-body-language-tips-for-2012/

32. Joseph Grenny, "Antisocial Networks? Hostility on social media rising for 78 percent of users." *Press Room*. Vital Smarts, 10 April, 2013, http://www. vitalsmarts.com/press/2013/04/antisocial-networks-hostility-on-social-media-rising-for-78-percent-of-users/

33. Yang, Dennis. "Tone Misinterpreted In Half Of All Emails | Techdirt." Techdirt. February 6, 2006. Accessed June 27, 2016. http://www.techdirt.com/articles/20060213/1558206.shtml

34. Staff. "Top 10 Funniest Text Messages from Parents." Techeblog Posts. March 17, 2012. Accessed June 27, 2016. http://www.techeblog.com/index.php/tech-gadget/top-10-funniest-text-messages-from-parents

35. Patel, Neil. How to Increase Your LinkedIn Engagement by 386%. Quick Sprout. December 19, 2013. Accessed May 27, 2016. https://www.quicksprout.com/2013/12/19/how-to-increase-linkedin-engagement-by-386/

36. LinkedIn Best Practices: Targeted Status Updates. LinkedIn Best Practices: Targeted Status Updates. June 25, 2012. Accessed May 27, 2016. http://www.slideshare.net/LImarketingsolutions/linked-in-targetedstatusupdatesbestpractices

37. LinkedIn Best Practices: Targeted Status Updates. LinkedIn Best Practices: Targeted Status Updates. June 25, 2012. Accessed May 27, 2016. http://www.slideshare.net/LImarketingsolutions/linked-in-targetedstatusupdatesbestpractices

38. LinkedIn. 15 Tips for Compelling Company Updates on LinkedIn. 15 Tips for Compelling Company Updates on LinkedIn. June 27, 2013. Accessed May 27, 2016. http://www.slideshare.net/LImarketingsolutions/15-tips-for-compelling-company-updates

39. Kolowich, Lindsay. The Best Time to Post on Facebook, Twitter, LinkedIn & Other Top Social Networks [Infographic]. The Best Time to Post on Facebook, Twitter, LinkedIn & Other Top Social Networks [Infographic]. February 5, 2015. Accessed May 27, 2016. http://blog.hubspot.com/marketing/social-media-post-best-times#sm.0013u49p4aksfou11l22r5uqbznj5

40. Susi, Michael. "Pursuing a Career of Purpose: A Story of Hustle, Ambition, and Yoga." LinkedIn Official Blog. March 7, 2016. Accessed May 25, 2016. https://blog.linkedin.com/2016/03/07/pursuing-a-career-of-purpose

41. Levy, Mitchell, "Successful LinkedIn Endorsement Promotion Case Study," *Mitchell Levy: Chief Investigator of Ahas*, August 28, 2013. Accessed June 6, 2016. http://www.mitchelllevy.com/blog/successful-linkedin-endorsement-promotion-case-study

42. Gross, Jenna. Forbes. May 6, 2016. Accessed June 30, 2016. http://www.forbes.com/sites/forbesagencycouncil/2016/05/06/social-selling-101-five-hacks-to-connect-with-customers-and-grow-your-business/#5507e3d21243

43. LinkedIn. "The Sophisticated Guide to Marketing on LinkedIn." Sophisticated Guide for Marketing. 2016. Accessed June 28, 2016. https://business.linkedin.com/marketing-solutions/c/14/1/sophisticated-guide-for-marketing

44. LinkedIn. "The Sophisticated Guide to Marketing on LinkedIn." Sophisticated Guide for Marketing. 2016. Accessed June 28, 2016. https://business.linkedin.com/marketing-solutions/c/14/1/sophisticated-guide-for-marketing

45. Bullas, Jeff. "6 Powerful Reasons Why You Should Include Images in Your Marketing - Infographic." Jeffbullas.com. 2012. Accessed June 29, 2016. http://www.jeffbullas.com/2012/05/28/6-powerful-reasons-why-you-should-include-images-in-your-marketing-infographic/

46. NeoMam Studios. "Why Do Infographics Make Great Marketing Tools." NeoMam Studios. 2012. Accessed June 29, 2016. http://neomam.com/blog/infographics-make-great-marketing-tools/

47. NeoMam Studios. "Why Do Infographics Make Great Marketing Tools." NeoMam Studios. 2012. Accessed June 29, 2016. http://neomam.com/blog/infographics-make-great-marketing-tools/

48. NeoMam Studios. "Why Do Infographics Make Great Marketing Tools." NeoMam Studios. 2012. Accessed June 29, 2016. http://neomam.com/blog/infographics-make-great-marketing-tools/

49. Neary, John. From Executive to Entrepreneur and Back with the Help of My LinkedIn Network. LinkedIn Official Blog. August 26, 2014. Accessed May 27, 2016. https://blog.linkedin.com/2014/08/26/from-executive-to-entrepreneur-and-back-with-the-help-of-my-linkedin-network

50. Beese, Jennifer. "How To Use LinkedIn For Business | Sprout Social." Sprout Social. June 01, 2015. Accessed June 28, 2016. http://sproutsocial.com/insights/how-to-use-linkedin-for-business/

51. Cisco. "Cisco Visual Networking Index: Forecast and Methodology, 2015–2020." Cisco. June 1, 2016. Accessed June 29, 2016. http://www.cisco.com/c/en/us/solutions/collateral/service-provider/visual-networking-index-vni/complete-white-paper-c11-481360.html

52. Premasinghe, Vijith. "Online Video Marketing Statistics 2016 - TOP 20 Trends You Need to Know to Win the Future." LinkedIn. December 1, 2015. Accessed June 28, 2016. https://www.linkedin.com/pulse/online-video-marketing-statistics-2016-top-20-you-need-premasinghe

53. Tousley, Scott. "107 Mind-Blowing Sales Statistics That Will Help You Sell Smarter." 107 Mind-Blowing Sales Statistics That Will Help You Sell Smarter. September 14, 2015. Accessed July 01, 2016. http://blog.hubspot.com/sales/sales-statistics#sm.0013u49p4aksfou11l22r5uqbznj5

54. LinkedIn, "Getting Started on Social Selling with LinkedIn," Page 12

55. LinkedIn, "Getting Started on Social Selling with LinkedIn," Page 15

56. LinkedIn, "8 Steps to Become a Top Seller Infographic," accessed May 19, 2016, https://content.linkedin.com/content/dam/me/business/en-us/sales-solutions/resources/images/infographics/8-steps-to-become-a-top-seller-infographic.jpg

57. Sexton, Koka. "Sales Strategy: 23 Facts about Buyers and Purchasing." Business Solutions on LinkedIn. August 24, 2014. Accessed June 29, 2016. https://business.linkedin.com/sales-solutions/blog/s/sales-strategy-23-facts-about-buyers-and-purchasing

58. Schwartzman, Eric. "How To Find the Best B2B Social Media Linkedin Groups." Social Media B2B. February 28, 2013. Accessed June 27, 2016. http://socialmediab2b.com/2013/02/b2b-social-media-best-linkedin-groups/

59. Hull, Mark. "Take the Work Out of Networking: Real Member Perspectives." LinkedIn Official Blog. May 18, 2015. Accessed May 25, 2016. https://blog.linkedin.com/2015/05/18/take-the-work-out-of-networking-real-member-perspectives

60. Lazzaroni, Deanna. "60 B2B Marketing Quotes, Stats, and Facts for the Modern Marketer." Business Solutions on LinkedIn. Published May 13, 2016. Accessed May 21, 2016. https://business.linkedin.com/marketing-solutions/blog/6/60-b2b-marketing-quotes-stats-and-facts-for-the-modern-marketer#

61. Moth, David. "94% of Businesses Say Personalisation Is Critical to Their Success." Econsultancy. April 22, 2013. Accessed June 28, 2016. https://econsultancy.com/blog/62583-94-of-businesses-say-personalisation-is-critical-to-their-success/

62. Lazzaroni, Deanna. "60 B2B Marketing Quotes, Stats, and Facts for the Modern Marketer." Business Solutions on LinkedIn. Published May 13, 2016. Accessed May 21, 2016. https://business.linkedin.com/marketing-solutions/blog/6/60-b2b-marketing-quotes-stats-and-facts-for-the-modern-marketer#

63. Seppala, Emma. "The Compassionate Mind." Association for Psychological Science. Accessed April 31, 2016. http://www.psychologicalscience.org/index.php/publications/observer/2013/may-june-13/the-compassionate-mind.html

64. Boniwell, Illona. "Positive Psychology UK." Accessed May 3, 2016. http://positivepsychology.org.uk/pp-theory/happiness/57-happiness-and-subjective-well-being.html.

65. "Why Content Goes Viral: What Analyzing 100 Million Articles Taught Us. | OkDork.com." OkDorkcom. April 21, 2014. Accessed June 28, 2016. http://okdork.com/2014/04/21/why-content-goes-viral-what-analyzing-100-millions-articles-taught-us/

66. Steven MacDonald, "Social Selling: 8 Ways to Sell More Using Social Media," *SuperOffice*, May 4, 2016, Accessed August 5, 2016, http://www.superoffice.com/blog/social-selling/

67. Steven MacDonald, "Social Selling: 8 Ways to Sell More Using Social Media," *SuperOffice*, May 4, 2016, Accessed August 5, 2016, http://www.superoffice.com/blog/social-selling/

68. Steven MacDonald, "Social Selling: 8 Ways to Sell More Using Social Media," *SuperOffice*, May 4, 2016, Accessed August 5, 2016, http://www.superoffice.com/blog/social-selling/

69. LinkedIn."National Bank of Canada Grows Net Sales With LinkedIn Sales Navigator," LinkedIn Sales Solution, 2013, Accessed May 20, 2016, https://business.linkedin.com/content/dam/business/sales-solutions/global/en_US/site/pdf/cs/linkedin-national-bank-of-canada-case-study-en-us.pdf

70. Harris, Meg. LinkedIn Changed My Life So I Could Help Families with Special Needs. LinkedIn Official Blog. May 13, 2015. Accessed May 27, 2016. https://blog.linkedin.com/2015/05/13/linkedin-changed-my-life-so-i-could-help-families-with-special-needs

71. LinkedIn. "Apptio Reaches Key Stakeholders with LinkedIn Sales Navigator," LinkedIn Sales Solutions, 2013, Accessed May 20, 2016, https://business.linkedin.com/content/dam/business/sales-solutions/global/en_US/site/pdf/cs/linkedin-apptio-case-study-en us.pdf

72. LinkedIn. "Sales Navigator Builds Pipeline Through Increased Lead Flow and Insights to Use When Reaching Out." LinkedIn Sales Solutions. 2013. Accessed July 15, 2016. https://business.linkedin.com/content/dam/business/sales-solutions/global/en_US/site/pdf/cs/linkedin-new-horizons-case-study-en-us.pdf

73. LinkedIn. "HP Case Study," LinkedIn Marketing Solutions, 2013, accessed May 24, 2016, https://business.linkedin.com/content/dam/business/marketing-solutions/global/en_US/site/subsites/content-marketing/pdf/linkedin_hp_followers_case_study_us_en_130613.pdf

74. LinkedIn. "LinkedIn on LinkedIn: How We Build Our Base of LinkedIn Premium Subscribers," LinkedIn Marketing Solutions, 2015, accessed May 24, 2016, https://business.linkedin.com/content/dam/business/marketing-solutions/global/en_US/site/pdf/cs/linkedin-lol-case-study.pdf

75. LinkedIn, "Seed Equity Attracts Investors to Startup Ventures with Spotlight Ads and Sponsored Updates," *LinkedIn Marketing Solutions*, 2016, accessed May 24, 2016, https://business.linkedin.com/marketing-solutions/resources/finance/seed-equity-cs

76. Schaffer, Neal, "How I Developed Business on LinkedIn — a LinkedIn Case Study," *Maximize Social Business*, August 23, 2015. Accessed June 6, 2016. http://maximizesocialbusiness.com/linkedin-b2b-business-development-case-study-4959/